MW00947312

Our Transplant Journey:
A Caregiver's Story

By

Ron Moore

Alisa –
Good luck with
your studies. I hope
this helps.

Ron Moore

Other books by Ron Moore

Making Common Sense Common Practice:
Models for Manufacturing Excellence

What Tool? When?
A Management Guide for
Selecting the Right Improvement Tools

The RM Group, Inc.
12024 Broadwood Drive
Knoxville, TN 37934, USA

Copyright © 2011, The RM Group, Inc. All rights reserved.

No part of this publication may be reproduced, stored in a retrieval system, or transmitted in any form or by any means, electronic, mechanical, photocopying, recording, or otherwise without the prior written permission of the publisher.

Permission may be sought directly from The RM Group, Inc., Phone: 1-865-675-7647.

ISBN-13: 978-1463505349

ISBN-10: 1463505345

Cover by Todd Schott, Knoxville, TN

Contents

About the Author

This book is dedicated to the memory of the donor
and the sacrifice of the donor family.
May you find comfort in knowing
that you have helped others to live.

Thank You

Our deepest gratitude goes to the donor and the donor family whose gift made the continuation of Kathy's life possible, and to all the medical personnel – doctors, physician's assistants, nurses, nurses assistants, and administrators – who helped with Kathy's transplant, pre-, during, and post-transplant. Words can hardly express this gratitude. We are in your debt until the final days of our lives, which have been so greatly extended by your generosity and efforts.

Our deep thanks also goes to friends and family who supported us through our transplant journey, especially Julia and Liz, Kathy's sisters, and their husbands for giving so freely of their time. Thanks to Sue and Lindelle and to Ron and Arlene for looking after our house when we moved temporarily to the Transplant Center. And thanks to all those whose thoughts and prayers encouraged and sustained us through it all.

Kathy is alive today through all your efforts.

Preface

Despair and elation are intense emotions at either end of the spectrum. Despair is a horrible feeling, even if it lasts only a moment. Elation is a wonderful feeling, even if it too lasts only a moment. We experienced both, several times, during our transplant journey.

The statistics are scary. Of all the people suffering from end-stage liver disease, some 10-15% die while waiting for a liver transplant. An additional 10-15% die during the first year after their transplant. An additional 10-15% die over the next four years. Overall, about 67% survive the first five years. One more sobering statistic is that 100% of the people with end-stage liver disease die if they *don't* receive a transplant. After those five years, you're more likely to die of something other than liver disease, hopefully old age. Many of these deaths are due to other complicating factors that increase the risk of death. These complications are numerous, but the most common seem to be cancer, diabetes, heart disease, lung disease, and obesity, or some combination of these. A healthy life style will minimize the risk of death from liver disease, including the complications that often go with the disease.

It has been a challenging, frightening, tearful, and even joyful journey so far with many ups and downs. The downs can be difficult, like Kathy's periods of encephalopathy (confusion) and aphasia (difficulty speaking). The really difficult times were periods like Kathy's critically low blood sodium which caused her brain stem swelling, a condition known as hyponatremia, which can be fatal, and temporarily took her off the transplant list; the waiting for the transplant; the grand mal seizure caused by one of the anti-rejection medications; the many biopsies to check for transplant rejection; and the post-discharge infections that required re-admission.

The whole process is gut-wrenching, like what I imagine it would feel like to go to hell and back. There were times when either one of us would feel a deep sense of despair, as if there was little hope. Fortunately, it never happened to both of us at the same time. Eating was a struggle for both of us on many days. Getting rest was a struggle on many days as well, even when others were helping. Having help from other family members, like Kathy's sisters, was a godsend. I don't really know how anyone would cope with all the unexpected things that happen without help.

While this book is about going through a liver transplant, the principles that my wife Kathy and I have learned in the course of her transplant, likely apply to any transplant, or in many cases to any major medical procedure. As the old saying goes, forewarned is forearmed, so we hope our sharing of our experience will help you in dealing with any major medical procedure you encounter. I'll also be using a few technical medical terms at least once, before converting them into every day language. The book is also written primarily from the view of a care giver, me in this case, so it's likely to be more useful to care givers. However, it should also be very helpful to transplant recipients, and to medical professionals, i.e., doctors, nurses, physician's assistants, and various technicians, who may want to consider changing their protocols to address the issues we cover. It's written as a narrative that describes the events as they occur, often day-to-day, and at times even moment-to-moment.

This book began as a series of notes to help me in my effort to be an advocate for Kathy as we worked together to help her cope with liver disease. I wanted to keep good records and notes of all the things that were ongoing so that I could better help her. These notes also included an ever-changing set of questions that I kept, sometimes on a piece of paper in my shirt pocket, to ask her doctors each time we saw them.

The notes were just that, notes, but as they accumulated, I began to recognize certain things that I didn't know beforehand, and more importantly would like to have known, so that I could have done a better job. Those notes slowly became the beginning of this book, one that I've written with the hope of helping others, first to survive; and then to minimize the risk to their health before and after any major medical procedure, but in particular those with end-stage liver disease; and finally, to help caregivers and close family members care for their loved one, who will need a strong advocate.

All in all, Kathy received excellent care. The doctors, nurses, technicians, administrators, and health insurance providers were all really good. I would not hesitate to recommend her health care providers to anyone in need of a transplant. That said, however, it's likely that if you're in need of a transplant, liver or otherwise, or receive major medical care, errors large and small will be made, most unknowingly. I made them, the doctors made them, the nurses made them, the technicians made them. In our case, these were not negligent errors, but rather were made with the best of intentions and typically following standard medical protocol. Unfortunately, as with most protocols, and with most people, there are sufficient differences in individuals that few protocols work exactly the same way for every person. And thus, constant vigilance is needed to catch any errors and to make changes when necessary, or when something isn't working. This also makes it essential that the patient and their caregivers be constantly alert to address subtle changes and differences that are critical to the ultimate success of the process. It also makes the habit of taking notes, asking questions, and generally being very disciplined and engaged in the health care process a critical part of the success of the procedure and ultimate recovery of the patient. I asked lots of questions *every time* we saw a doctor.

For husbands/wives and other caregivers, be prepared to wash and wipe areas you wouldn't ordinarily wash and wipe; to clean up vomit; to brush teeth; to trim finger and toe nails; to put on ointment; to give leg rubs, arm rubs, and neck rubs; to clean feces and urine, to clean wounds and scabs, to nurse, to wipe tears, to cry tears, to hurt, to lose sleep, to be very, very tired, and still go on because you love them so. If you have qualms about any of this, get over it. You'll need to do it, and in a very clinical manner. Your spouse or significant other will need every ounce of support you can give. And, be prepared to be very, very patient. Your spouse or loved one will be very tired, hurting a lot, at times very cranky and impatient. They may lose contact with reality through encephalopathy and aphasia. Be prepared to respond to any hurtful comment with a hug, a kiss and a smile, and a response that affirms your commitment to help him/her (and you) get through this.

All this has to be done while paying bills, cleaning house, cooking and washing dishes, doing laundry, putting things away, helping him or her get bathed and dressed; and perhaps even working and keeping up with your "day job". And, you have to respond to friends, family and well wishers who care for you and are concerned. At times however, this can be overwhelming. There were times when I simply didn't want to talk to anyone about anything. I even wrote a note advising people that yes, we wanted them to call, but if we didn't answer, we were probably doing something, i.e., cleaning, feeding, bathing, dressing, meds, talking with doctors, nurses, nurses aids, doing PT or OT or speech therapy, or talking with others, or simply resting. I promised to call back when I could. It is, as you can see, a very busy and difficult period.

We found that individual doctors are often not "systems thinkers". While not an absolute truth, each specialist doctor naturally tends to approach the patient from the view of his or her specialty. A hepatologist sees your liver; a cardiologist sees your heart; a gastroenterologist sees your intestinal tract; a hematologist sees your blood, and so on.

Having worked with hundreds of manufacturers, I've often observed the same sort of behavior there. Production thinks about production, maintenance thinks about maintenance, marketing thinks about marketing, accounting thinks about accounting. While there is nothing inherently wrong with this, and it has many good attributes, it can and often does lead to a dysfunctional system, because each function is only considering its function, and not looking at the impact of its decisions on the system as a whole. Manufacturers tend to optimize at the sub-optimal level. One of my jobs is to get them to work as a team, aligning and integrating their functions for the greater good of the entire business.

Likewise, this can be true for the medical profession. At times one specialist can make recommendations and orders that are inconsistent or even contrary to another specialist. I'm glad to report that Kathy's transplant team did a much better job at integrating the various recommendations into a systems level view, primarily because they worked as a team with each specialist communicating his or her recommendations to the other in an effort to achieve a consensus approach. That said, they were not perfect, and more broadly speaking, our experience has been that at times doctors do not think about the patient at a systems level, that is considering all the treatments and risks simultaneously. It's often critical that they answer the question – "What are the implications of each treatment, taken collectively, on the patient as a whole?

We also found that our insurance company was very helpful, not the money-hungry underhanded demons that so many in the movies, national news media, and politics want to portray them. In fact they were quite the opposite, being very caring and helpful. They did, of course, advise us about what was covered under our policy and what was not. They covered what they said they would cover, and did not cover what they said they would not. That's fair. Any time we had a question, they were very responsive in providing detailed and accurate information.

Clearly they have an obligation to all their customers to contain costs, while providing the best service possible within the limits of those costs. To do otherwise would be foolish, and they would not be in business to provide any service at all. They must also charge fees consistent with the level of coverage, and risk, that their customers can afford and are willing to take. It is not realistic for anyone, particularly the media, or my least favorite, movie stars speaking from a position of ignorance, to expect that everything will be available to everyone, no matter the cost. We all pay eventually, so we must individually become active participants in managing our own health care.

Because of our employment situation, we have individual policies with very high deductibles and co-pays, making it expensive to get sick, something we have known all along, and more importantly something for which we were prepared by putting aside a large emergency fund. I am not a supporter of free health care, since it is not free, and only encourages those who consider it "free" to misuse the system, making it ultimately unsustainable. Checks and balances, accountability, and transparency, are essential in any properly functioning system, but especially in health care.

With Kathy's full support, it is my intent to share with you our experience with the hope that you will benefit from that and improve the probability of a successful outcome for you. Thank you for allowing us to share it with you. I'll be using names that are disguised, such as Dr. S or Dr. B, since I don't want to identify her physicians, and I think they have all done a good job with the information they had. Specifically, I don't see any malpractice at all on their part. Quite the contrary, for the most part I see them as very competent physicians doing the best job they could with the information and training they have.

I'll also be using the generic names of the medications that were used in treating Kathy. It's just easier than having to use the trade names and listing them as trademarked. A listing of the medications with both trade and corresponding generic names is provided in Appendix A, so you can cross check these if needed. You can go on line to find lots of additional information about each of them, including side effects and interactions, something that everyone is encouraged to review in detail. Incidentally, as you will see, drug side effects and interactions are something that I did not initially give nearly enough attention. It gets plenty of attention now.

Further, most of what I'll share with you is based on my notes, research and memory, and is as accurate as I can make it, but some of it may be faulty at times. There is no intention to mislead at all, and I welcome any comments that would make the story more accurate. In any event, please don't take this book as being absolutely accurate, but rather as a guide to help you sort through those issues that may be important to you.

Finally, this is a kind of love story. Not the gushy, infatuated love that we sometimes see, or even feel, but the deep love that sustains one through the most difficult of times, as any transplant journey will be. If you're a caregiver for someone having a transplant, you'll find that you will have to do things you didn't imagine before. At least I did. And, the effort will require more than you thought it would, maybe even more than you thought you could tolerate. It's critical that you take care of yourself, so you can take care of your loved one. One of the most important things you can do is take it all *one day at a time.*

Ron Moore
Knoxville, Tennessee

The Beginning – A Fatty Liver

1

The truth is we don't know when this journey began. For several years Kathy was referred to as having a "fatty liver". Ultimately, I learned that it is commonly a reversible condition wherein large vacuoles of triglyceride fat accumulate in the liver. It is most commonly associated with people who consume excess alcohol or are obese. Kathy does not drink, nor is she obese. It is also associated with other diseases that influence fat metabolism. As we will learn, Kathy fits into the later category.

In any event, she routinely had higher than normal liver enzymes, so-called AST and ALT in particular (aspartate aminotransferase and alanine aminotransferase, respectively, for those interested – they help create proteins in the blood). If the liver is injured or diseased, the liver spills the enzymes into the blood, raising the enzyme levels and indicating potential liver damage. But according to the doctors, these enzymes do not correlate well with the extent of liver damage, and so cannot be used to judge the degree of liver disease or predict the future. So, many years ago we began the watchful waiting period regarding her liver.

At some point Kathy's family doctor, Dr. M, recommended that she see a specialist, likely because he saw a substantial change in the results of her liver panel blood test. We saw Dr. G for one visit and he had an initial diagnosis, but soon thereafter she was no longer covered by our insurance company, and she transferred to Dr. B. Somewhere around 2003, Dr. B diagnosed Kathy as having autoimmune hepatitis, a degenerative disease of the liver. I did some limited research to find that the nominal life span of someone with this condition was about seven years from the initial diagnosis. It was a frightening and sad moment, but surprisingly not something we discussed very much. Maybe if we ignored it, it would go away. Our watchful waiting continued. He prescribed nadalol, a blood pressure medication to reduce the pressure on the varices to her liver, and thus minimize the risk of bleeding, and said to see him every 6-12 months. It was all very clinical, even to us.

When I asked about what we should do next, Kathy always said "There's nothing we can do". I presumed this was what she had been told by Dr. B. We muddled along for years, but it was obvious that Kathy was ever so slowly feeling worse and growing weaker. Her decline was imperceptible month to month, but it was clear from one year to the next that she was getting weaker – she had less enthusiasm for visiting with the kids and grandkids either at their homes or ours, had less enthusiasm for our physical relationship, and was slowly withdrawing from being the Kathy that I had known and loved for decades. It was very difficult for me. At one point I said to her, in a moment of frustration, "I just want to my Kathy back." Little did I know it would be years before I had her back.

Chasing Diabetes

2

Our liver transplant journey began in earnest on November 5, 2008 in Huntsville, Alabama. I was there on a project for a local chemical company and Kathy had decided to join me, since we had two kids and three grandkids that lived there. I could work, and she/we could visit. It was a nice trip. We had dinner planned at one of our daughter's house on Wednesday night.

That day I called Kathy at the hotel before leaving the plant just to confirm our plans for dinner. She sounded tired, even lethargic. I told her I'd see her in a few minutes, cheerily said "I love you", and hung up. When I arrived at the hotel, she was half dressed, lying on the bed, seemed to be half asleep, and could not talk. She could not walk or even sit up. She was cold and clammy. Checking for signs of a stroke, I asked her to raise both arms above her head. She did, and they rose uniformly. I asked her to stick out her tongue. She did, and it did *not* go to one side. I asked her to say Peter Piper picked a peck of pickled peppers. Very slowly and softly, she said, "Peter Piper picked a peh, peh, peh…" Though she couldn't get the last words out, I didn't think she'd had a stroke.

I quickly decided to take her to the emergency room, but she could not walk, and began to cry when I tried to get her to sit up. She seemed mentally confused. I didn't know the meaning of the word encephalopathy (mental confusion) at the time, but in the coming months we would come to know this word very well, since she would experience this condition several times in the coming year.

I called Liz, her sister and a nurse, and told her about Kathy and the tests I had done. All I remember of that conversation was "Call an ambulance and get to an ER." While we were waiting, I helped Kathy get dressed. It was like getting an unconscious body into clothing. The fire truck arrived first, with three or four large firemen in full gear. Kathy sat in dazed wonder at these large men giving her all this attention. Kathy's blood pressure was low – her diastolic blood pressure (the smaller number) was not detectable. They also administered a glucose (blood sugar) test and found that she had a reading 58. A normal fasting level is about 100. Soon thereafter, the ambulance arrived, and the EMT's did some routine field tests. Their initial diagnosis was hypoglycemia, or low blood sugar or glucose level, and they administered a large dose of sucrose. Kathy almost immediately began to feel better.

I was not allowed to ride in the ambulance with her, but caught up with her in the emergency room at the hospital. On the way I called the kids to let them know that we were on the way to the hospital, and our dinner plans were cancelled. I'd keep them posted. When I arrived, there was no room in the emergency room for her, so she was on a gurney in the hallway. She seemed normal now. The doctor concluded that she had a hypoglycemic incident. He discharged her and we went home. By then it was nearly 11pm.

At this point we were very concerned that she had developed or was developing diabetes, but were not sure what to do, so we decided to go to an endocrinologist for further evaluation and tests. In the interim, we began a diabetic diet, just in case, focusing on eating foods with a low glycemic index. These foods don't turn to sugar as rapidly in the blood, and allow the body to better manage and keep blood glucose levels more stable.

In retrospect, her encephalopathy from the hypoglycemic episode may have been because of poor liver function. The liver and pancreas are intertwined, affecting one another and inducing symptoms that could be either. For example, the liver stores glycogen, which is released as needed to convert to glucose in the blood. Kathy had eaten very little that day, "saving herself", for the evening meal, which she anticipated would be large. If her liver was not functioning properly, it likely was unable to store the glycogen needed for sustaining her during a period when she was not eating.

On January 26, 2009 we met with Dr. W, an endocrinologist, who specializes in the diagnosis and treatment of diabetes, and he ordered a series of tests. We also began taking her blood glucose level two or three times per day for him. During the consultation, we also advised him that Kathy had been diagnosed with autoimmune hepatitis. He asked when her biopsy was done, to which we replied that she hasn't had one. He observed that autoimmune hepatitis cannot be diagnosed without a biopsy. This surprised us, since Dr. B had made the diagnosis, but without any biopsy. This was the first of many lessons that we learned during our journey. I'll be describing these lessons, some 50 of them, at the end of the book, while mentioning several along the way.

He also indicated that she may have Type 2 diabetes, sometimes called adult onset diabetes, which can be controlled with diet and exercise. The tests continued, including a glucose tolerance test. Kathy also continued to do daily monitoring of her blood sugar, usually before breakfast, resulting in readings that were typically around 80, which is within the normal range. At the end of it all, Dr. W concluded that Kathy was not diabetic, but could develop diabetes. He referred us to Dr. S, a gastroenterologist.

Since he also indicated that diabetes can be controlled with diet and exercise, and that a healthy diet and exercise are good for you anyway, we began to exercise, mostly walking. We even bought two treadmills so we could walk together, listening to the Rolling Stones or Kool and the Gang, Kathy's favorites, though I prefer Bluegrass/Country or Bocelli, an odd mix of musical styles. At this point Kathy was in a weakened state, and did the exercises somewhat reluctantly. This was frustrating for me, since I exercise routinely. I would only realize later how weak she really was, and that she was in fact doing her best.

Diagnostics and Decline 3

On February 24, 2009, we had our first consultation with Dr. S. The place looked familiar, and we concluded that Kathy had seen Dr. G, an associate of Dr. S some years ago, but had switched to Dr. B, because of changes to her insurance policy which made Dr. G "out of network". He noted that based on Kathy's old file, years ago he would have put her on two medications – ursodiol and colchesine, and that there were clear indictors for doing this in the last entry to her file, which was several years old. At this point Dr. S prescribed both these for Kathy, believing she may have primary biliary cirrhosis. He also indicated that he had at least one patient who had returned to normal after several months on these medications. He indicated, among many possibilities of the diseases that Kathy could have, were primary biliary cirrhosis and hemachromatosis, the later of which would require more testing to affirm or reject as a diagnosis. We left Dr. S's office feeling better than we had in several years about Kathy's prospects. At least he was being active in her treatment, unlike her previous doctor.

During one of our visits to Dr. S, we related that Dr. M, our long-time family doctor, had prescribed for Kathy a low dose of zolpidem for sleeping, and a low dose of citalopram, an antidepressant. Pending a more comprehensive diagnosis, Dr. M indicated that Kathy's symptoms were characteristic of someone who is depressed. He indicated that if it turned out that it wasn't necessary, we could take her off the medication very easily and that the risk of her taking it was very low. It was a kind of "It might help, but it won't hurt" approach.

Kathy had told Dr. M, that if she were a man, he wouldn't prescribe this. He took great exception to her assertion. I recall the full version of "BS" being said, along with other admonitions. And so, she went on citalopram. In retrospect, I believe the symptoms related to her liver disease are similar to those for depression, that is, a prolonged period sleeplessness, lack of energy, loss of appetite, irritability, and so on. And, Kathy had previously been on citalopram during a very difficult period in our lives, when both our fathers died within months of each other, and our son Jake, who is handicapped, developed pancreatitis and nearly died, among other difficult events.

After describing all this, I asked Dr. S, if, given her liver condition, it was ok for her to continue with the low dose of sleeping pill and anti-depressant. He said there shouldn't be a problem in the doses indicated. Little did I know how significant this would become . He was also concerned about her liver condition and wanted to get a more comprehensive review of its function. So, he ordered a liver biopsy and an ERCP (endoscopic retrograde cholangiopancreatography for those interested in the technical term). The ERCP uses a small scope with a camera to go down the esophagus through the stomach and into the intestine to further check her bile duct, pancreatic duct, and liver condition.

In early March 2009, Kathy had a biopsy of her liver that required anesthesia. Most liver biopsies are done using a needle, but her platelet count was very low, increasing the risk of excessive bleeding, likely because of her liver disease. Because of this low platelet count, they decided a lower risk approach would be to go through her carotid artery and down into her liver to get the tissue sample for the biopsy. She also had a triphasic spiral CT scan of her liver to check its size and general condition, and the vessels leading to it.

Later that week, the ERCP was done, also requiring anesthesia, and indicating her varices were enlarged. As a result of all these tests, Dr. S concluded that her MELD score was quite low at the time, that is, she was not sick enough to be listed for a transplant.

This was my introduction to the MELD score, or Model for End-stage Liver Disease. It is a measure of the liver's function and in case you're interested it's calculated as follows:

MELD = (3.78 x Ln(B)) + (11.2 x Ln(INR)) + (9.57 x Ln(C)) + 6.43

Where:
>   Ln = Natural Log

>   B = Bilirubin, mg/dl; a fluid that aids in digestion and is secreted by the liver.

>   INR = A clotting factor (International Normalized Ratio) that is the ratio between the coagulation time of a sample of blood and the normal coagulation time, when coagulation takes place in certain standardized conditions.

>   C = Creatinine, mg/dl; A chemical waste molecule that is generated from muscle metabolism. The kidneys filter out most of the creatinine and dispose of it in the urine. Although it is a waste, creatinine serves a vital diagnostic function and has been found to be a fairly reliable indicator of kidney function.

My impression from this was that the kidneys can be impacted by the liver function and so kidney function is a key indicator of liver function.

At this point you may be getting more information than you really need, so feel free to ignore those parts that aren't necessary to you and your plans. However, it is essential to understand that the MELD score is used as the basis for determining a patient's priority on the waiting list for a liver transplant. That is, the higher the MELD score, the sicker the patient is considered to be, and the higher priority they have on the transplant list.

We found out later that the MELD score is also an indication of mortality risk in the next 90 days for a given patient. For example, according to one source, if your MELD score is 10, your risk of dying within 90 days is 4%; at 15, it's 13%; at 20 it's 25%; at 25 it's 43%; and at 30 it's 62%; at 40 it's nearly 100%. Other sources indicate the probability of death is lower than this, so this appears to be the maximum risk. Unfortunately, as we found, as time passes the deterioration continues and can accelerate, increasing the MELD score, and the risk of death. So, the MELD score is not a measure that is static. It will typically increase with time, but over short periods (say a few weeks) can actually decrease, most likely due to the variation inherent in the measurement itself, and due to the normal variation in day-to-day body function.

During the ensuing six months of testing and evaluation for actually getting Kathy listed for the transplant, her MELD score went from less than 10 to 17 to 23, and then within a week to 28.

The transplant center indicated they generally did transplants when the individual's MELD score was between 17 and 23. My impression of this is that they want to do the surgery when you're at substantial risk of dying, but not so sick that you won't survive the surgery and recovery period. It seems to be a delicate and risky balance they're trying to strike.

In any event, a couple of days after Kathy's biopsy and ERCP in March, during both of which she was anesthetized, I had a business trip scheduled to Australia. Historically, it has taken her a few days to completely eliminate the effects of the anesthesia. And, recall that she was also taking a low dose sleeping pill, and on a low dose of anti-depressant, with her doctor's approval. She was not doing very well. She was weak, tired all the time and had little appetite. Because of all this, while I was gone to Australia, we reserved a flight for her to go to her sister Julia's in Florida where Julia could help with her care. In retrospect, that was *not* the right decision.

The morning of my departure, Kathy seemed to be having difficulty paying attention to the most trivial of tasks. For example, she had trouble getting the pillows onto the bed while we were making it, but I simply dismissed this in my mind as her being distracted by my departure. I found out later that she had gone to the airport shortly after I left, but her flight was the *next* day. She was embarrassed by this, particularly when the check-in clerk told her, "Mrs. Moore, your flight isn't until *tomorrow* at this time." More critically, the next day while she was driving to the airport she ran over a curb and had a blowout, but wasn't truly aware of it. She drove several miles on a blown-out tire and did some $1,200 in damage to the car.

Recall that she had been anesthetized twice in the prior week, and was still taking a low dose of sleeping medication and an anti-depressant. Looking back, the combination of these medications with end-stage liver disease could have been a disastrous combination for Kathy. She could have been killed.

While I was in Australia, I was in touch with Julia daily. Kathy was sleeping 18-20 hours per day, was having difficulty talking, and was generally lethargic. Encephalopathy was also rearing its ugly head.

Notwithstanding Dr. S and Dr. M's approval of it, and considering the lingering effects of the anesthesia the week before, Julia and I decided to take her off both the sleeping pill and anti-depressant. We believed her liver was simply not processing these two medications and that they were accumulating in her blood, resulting in the lethargy and need to sleep all the time. Within a few days after we did this, she improved markedly in energy and cognition, but was still very tired and had little appetite. Another lesson was learned regarding medications.

From this point I'll be doing a specific chronological review of the events by date, and at some point will go to a day-to-day review, even moment-to-moment.

April 8 – At Dr. S's suggestion, I begin to keep a log book of all the food Kathy is consuming at each meal. For *each* item eaten, I begin weighing it on a food scale and tracking all her protein, fat, carbohydrates and calories consumed. Dr. S wants to make sure that based on her weight, she gets a minimum of 40 grams of protein per day to minimize muscle loss, but no more than about 45 grams to minimize ammonia buildup in her bloodstream and cause encephalopathy.

It's a fine balance to strike and it's a lot of work, a very time consuming effort. While most of this information is provided on the packaging of processed foods, we eat a lot of fresh fruits and vegetables and other unpackaged foods, and we often have to look things up on the internet. For example, how many calories, protein, fat, and carbs are in a half cup of blueberries? An ounce of cheese? A cup of broccoli? An apple? And so on. Moreover, all this must be logged and added to get the total consumption of each on e, every day.

We also continue to focus on minimizing foods with a high sugar content, and to maximize foods with a low glycemic index and high fiber content, so that we minimize the risk of diabetes during her illness. Incidentally, we learn during this time that foods with high fiber also tend to help reduce the glycemic index and thus are healthier, helping minimize the risk of diabetes. We do not want yet another complication to add to her liver disease.

It will turn out later that keeping this log is *critical* to maintaining Kathy's overall health and to assuring she can function at a minimal level as she continues to decline. As the liver deteriorates, its ability to process protein also apparently deteriorates. Striking the right balance, that is, not too much protein such that she becomes encephalopathic, and not so little that her muscle mass essentially disappears, will become increasingly difficult. Measuring and managing this will become a first order of business for us. A sample of one of her daily dietary log sheets is shown in Appendix B, while Appendix C provides an example of a monthly summary of her daily food consumption. Since I was doing it for her, I also began a log book on my food consumption as well.

To help us better manage Kathy's health, we also began consulting with a professional dietician, Kayla. She was excellent, having exceptional knowledge about the body's various systems and functions and how food interacts with those. She helped us tremendously with getting the balance right, finding foods Kathy could eat and would like (a difficult task), and generally helping with maintaining a minimum level of nutrition, given 1) her end-stage liver disease, and 2) a continuing concern about the possibility of her developing diabetes. During this period Kathy's appetite is very whimsical, and on some days is non-existent, making it hard to understand and plan what she might eat.

April 9 – We see Dr. S who says that Kathy's blood work indicates her enzymes are improving some, but we need to continue with the medication and observation. This gives us some hope that she's improving. Now that the medications for sleeping and depression are completely out of her system, she also seems to be feeling better, and to have slightly more energy. We're hopeful.

Somewhere around this time, Kathy also develops a habit of chewing on ice, constantly. It seems it gives her some relief from the struggle of day-to-day living. I'm not sure if it's a distraction from those problems, or simply a habit. It annoys me to no end, hearing the constant crunch, crunch, crunch. I try not to say much, being considerate of her feelings, but it becomes a bit like someone dragging their fingernails across a chalk board. Sometimes I simply leave the room. I do keep her supplied with ice, even if it bugs me. I tolerate it as best I can. This habit will go on for months, but I never quite get used to it. Eventually it does stop. I mention this to let everyone know that if you're a care giver, there will likely be things your loved one does that irritate you to no end. Please tolerate it and sympathize with it, so long as it isn't harmful. For Kathy it was one of the few things that gave her some comfort, and she needed my support in getting what little comfort she could have.

It was also somewhere around this time that I begin to do essentially all the cooking, housework, chores, shopping, yard work, and all the day-to-day activities around most households. I do this while still working at my regular job, recognizing that at some point it would be put on hold. When I do have to travel on business, Liz and Charlie, her sister and brother-in-law and both nurses, stay with her. For that I'm very grateful.

All in all, however, it is very difficult trying to keep up with everything. I remind myself to take things one day at a time. Indeed, after we knew that Kathy would need a transplant, I would constantly use phrases in our conversation like "We're going to get through this, one day at a time.", or, "This too shall pass." It helps.

Moreover, during this time, Kathy's ability to do our daily walk, or much of any exercise, slowing deteriorates. Some days she can barely walk a quarter of a mile, and that only at a very slow pace. It is very difficult for me to see her, once a bundle of energy and enthusiasm, have so little energy. She struggles on to do as much as she can. I try to be patient, sometimes unsuccessfully.

April 20 – We see Dr. W regarding her status as to diabetes, and we tell him that her enzymes seem to be improving. Dr. W notes presciently that she may be in full liver failure, that is, her liver is beginning to slow or even stop producing the enzymes because it is failing. He motions with his hands the picture of a hill, observing that as the enzymes increase, we know the liver is not well, but as the enzymes decline, it could mean that we are on the downward slope of the hill, moving toward failure, not back toward recovery. It's an easy mental picture to grasp, but also discouraging. The good news is that with all the tests that have been done he concludes that she is not diabetic. He encourages us to continue with the low glycemic index diet to minimize the risk in the future.

May 5 – We see Dr. S again, and he acknowledges that Kathy could be in liver failure, not improving as we had hoped. We continue with the medication and treatment he has prescribed. He also advises Kathy to get vaccinated for hepatitis A and B to minimize the risk of infection in her weakened state. We do this on May 7.

He seems to be very pleased that we are tracking in detail all Kathy's food consumption. He thinks that if Kathy does need a transplant, this will demonstrate our discipline in following directions and will make the transplant center more likely to approve her for a transplant. This adds to our motivation to do all the work necessary keeping track of this. It continues to be a lot of work.

May 10 – I leave for Australia for business today, but I'm very concerned about Kathy's health. Knowing that Liz and Charlie will be with her while I'm gone gives me some comfort. I call daily, sometimes twice, to check on her. During those conversations, it seems to me that Kathy is getting progressively worse. My fears are well founded.

May 14 – Kathy is admitted to hospital with severe encephalopathy and aphasia, that is, confusion and an inability to speak clearly. This has been induced by a blood ammonia level of 167, and she apparently is not very tolerant of this level.

I rush home from Perth, Australia, on the direct opposite side of the globe, but it's hard to "rush" when you're so far away. I finally get home the night of May 16 and go straight to the hospital. Kathy is doing and feeling much better and we have a pleasant reunion, and a discussion with Dr. S. With this most recent event of encephalopathy, Dr. S advises us that Kathy is in fact in end-stage liver disease and needs a liver transplant. *Our hope for any kind of recovery is dashed.*

Over the next few days, we review all the options available. Some transplant centers are not covered by our insurance. Others, including our first choice, are only partially covered and there we're likely looking at $200,000 out of pocket.

So we begin to consider the five "centers of excellence" transplant centers that are covered by our insurance company.

After looking on-line at the number of transplants each one does, their success rates, and doing some general research, and talking with Dr. S, he recommends one of these and we accept his judgment on this.

He has worked with several patients who have had, or need, a transplant, and so we believe his experience and judgment are critical in our decision making. One key point in the decision making, and in his recommendation, is that many patients die while waiting for a transplant. One of the causes of this, beyond perhaps individual complications, appears to be a lower supply of donors in the area of the transplant center. So, he has recommended a transplant center where they seem to do more transplants because of a better supply of donors, and they have good statistics on the outcomes following the transplant – they are better than or at least as good as the national averages. We agree with his recommendation and he provides a referral for us. We follow up by making an appointment at the transplant center.

I still don't understand the reasons for one area to have a better supply of donors, but *encourage everyone to become a donor*. You never know when you may have the opportunity to save a life, even in your death, and the families will be eternally grateful, as we are. Kathy and I are donors, and were, long before she needed a transplant.

June 8 – We receive a "Green Book", or Adult Liver Transplant Center Manual, which contains all kinds of information, including detailed information regarding what we should do and expect prior to and after a transplant, and the many risks involved. I read every page, line for line, and identify many questions that I want to ask.

I also visit several web sites regarding liver disease and transplant centers. In reading this manual, we also understand that she will have to undergo many additional tests, including, but not limited to a chest X-ray, electrocardiogram (EKG), pulmonary function test, echocardiogram, and possibly an adenosine myoview heart scan.

Other tests may also be necessary, depending on the results of these tests. In the coming weeks, Kathy will go through these, and more. It is both encouraging in tone, and discouraging, since the risks are many, both with the tests, and the transplant. It provides a realistic view of the things to come, but the only real way to truly understand these things is to actually experience them. We will.

At this point, I essentially stop working. I have a couple of one-day workshops or meetings in June and July that I do, but Liz and Charlie look after Kathy on those days. I contact all my customers and let them know I won't be available until the first quarter of 2010, at the earliest. Kathy and I have been self-employed for several years, and we've always understood that if one of us became seriously ill, then our income could come to a screeching halt. So, we prepared for this possibility by saving enough to get us through a long illness. We're both glad that we did.

The Gray List –
Multiple Tests and
Conflicting Instructions

4

June 15 – We have our first consultation with Dr. Z at the transplant center. He seems very competent, but is not very personable. He's a bit like the TV character "House", though not as caustic. That also seems to clash with my pedantic approach and wanting detail, and my military background. I have a list of 25 questions to ask, and when he finally concludes with his questions and review, he asks if we have any questions. So, I pull out my list. He rolls his eyes. This does not sit well with me, but I carry on, noting that he has already answered most of my questions. My first question is "Why should we come here?" to which he responds "I'm not in marketing". My reply is that I'm not interested in being marketed, but I do want to understand the steps they take to make sure the outcomes are as good as they can be with the patients they have. What I'd really like to know is "Would you have a transplant done here?" Rather than answer either question, he gives us a web site that provides statistical data on their performance compared to other transplant centers. It is a web site I had already visited, and understand that they have a good track record. I suppose I'm just looking for some affirmation.

During our session with Dr. Z, we tell him that Dr. S has Kathy on a low protein diet, one that limits her to about 40 grams of protein per day.

Dr. S's concern is that excess protein could cause Kathy's blood ammonia levels to increase and induce another round of encephalopathy and aphasia. Simultaneously, Dr. S wants to make sure Kathy get sufficient protein to minimize muscle mass loss while she is waiting for a transplant. Dr. Z says he doesn't track protein and doesn't express any interest in it. This was surprising, but since he was a liver specialist, we put more credibility in his opinion. It may have been misplaced.

After it's all said and done Kathy and I both want Dr. Z to be Kathy's doctor, her hepatologist, for the transplant. He seems very competent, even if his personality leaves something to be desired. She asks me to "please don't piss him off." Dr. Z tells us for the first time that Kathy's MELD Score is 17 and he puts Kathy on the "gray list". This is apparently a list of people who are *trying to qualify* to be listed for a transplant. Once on the transplant list, your priority is determined by your MELD score. If your MELD score is highest in your blood group, you're number one on the list in that group, and you will be offered the next liver available that is a match for you. The characteristics of that donor and their liver are also provided to you, and you can turn the offer down. My impression is that most do not.

After seeing Dr. Z, we meet with a nurse coordinator who is our point of contact for all the procedures that Kathy will have to go through prior to any transplant. In fact, these tests and procedures seem to be designed to make sure you're a good candidate for a transplant and to address any problems or complications that are identified before the transplant. We'll look more at these later.

We also meet with a financial advisor, not in the personal financial planning sense, but rather one who reviews our insurance coverage and advises us of our potential out-of-pocket costs.

They are substantial, ranging anywhere from $35,000-65,000 per year, since Kathy has no coverage for medications, including the anti-rejection medications post transplant, which are very expensive. These will likely be the bulk of our out-of-pocket costs. We tell the financial advisor that we're prepared to cover those expenses. We have individual policies and are already aware of Kathy's deductibles, and potential out-of-pocket and medication expenses. We began a long time ago preparing for a situation similar to this.

The nurse coordinator advises us, as the Green Book had indicated, that Kathy will have to undergo a series of tests to qualify for a transplant. After those tests are complete, the transplant team will meet and decide if she will be placed on the list. If she is, she will be given a number, based on her MELD score, that determines her priority for a transplant in her blood group. If your number is one, then you're first on the list for a transplant; two, then you're second, and so on. It's very scary to think that she might not qualify to be placed on the list, since that means certain death with her end-stage liver disease. The nurse also arranges for tests to be conducted on July 1 and 2, and consistent with the Green Book, advises us to get a hepatitis A and B shot and booster, along with a pneumonia shot and a TB test. She stresses that *no live virus inoculations of any kind are permitted*, as they apparently increase the risk of infection and death to a person with end-stage liver disease.

We're also advised that the waiting period after you're placed on the list can be several weeks, if not months, and for some it may be a year or more. And, we have to be ready at a moment's notice to report to the hospital for a transplant. Unfortunately, we live several hours from the Transplant Center traveling mostly on interstate highways.

Considering the potential for delays in being notified, the potential for delays because of heavy traffic or accidents on the interstate, we don't want to be that far away, if and when we get the call that she has a donor. It just seems too risky to us. Kathy's life is at stake. Moreover, the post-op treatment requires that we be nearby for several months, allowing for routine blood work, checkups, rehabilitation, and for quick access to the doctors if any problems develop that require hospitalization. This is particularly important in the first few weeks after discharge, since it is very common for a transplant patient to require re-hospitalization after discharge to address potential issues such as rejection, infection, adjustment of medications, or some combination of these. This will turn out to be true for Kathy as well.

Because of all this we decide that after Kathy is officially on the transplant list that we will move into an apartment near the Transplant Center, and live there awaiting the call and for the post discharge treatment. So, after researching furnished apartments on the internet for that area, we make a list of criteria we want in an apartment and arrange to visit several that are nearby during one of our trips.

It takes a full day to visit all the apartments on our list. After this, we eliminate some and develop a list of the remaining ones in order of preference. So, once we decide to move, we can contact those based on our priority until we select the apartment we want. One of the criteria I have for the apartment complex we select is that it must have a small gym or fitness center. I wanted to stay in good physical condition so that I could better support Kathy. So, regular workouts of walking, jogging, and general fitness are essential.

As it turned out, working out, usually while Kathy was napping, was very therapeutic for me. It soon became a regular part of my day. More importantly, Kathy would join me as much as she could to do as much as she was physically able. This would benefit her later as she worked to recover.

One thing that we found very encouraging was asking the nurses if they would come to this Transplant Center for a transplant, or send their loved ones here. They both said "of course", and in fact spoke glowingly of the Transplant Center. My experience has been that if you really want to know what's happening in a medical institution, ask the people who do the day-to-day work of taking care of patients and working directly with the doctors and other technicians. They, the nurses, are in the best position to offer an objective opinion on the quality of care. We will, in fact, later be very impressed by the nursing staff at the Transplant Center hospital.

July 1-2 – Kathy and I return to the Transplant Center for a series of tests, mostly blood work. As I recall they took 17 vials of blood for testing any number of things, such as liver function, kidney function, nutritional status, comprehensive red blood and white blood count, blood clotting ability, HIV, alcohol and other drugs, among other tests. We're also advised again that Kathy must get pneumonia and tetanus/diphtheria vaccinations, a test for tuberculosis, and hepatitis A and B vaccinations. We tell the nurse that she has already had a hepatitis A and B shot on May 7, at the direction of Dr. S, and is scheduled for a booster in July.

The nurse coordinator also wants to know if Kathy has had a recent colonoscopy, so that it will not have to be repeated as part of the pre-screening for being listed for a transplant. Fortunately for us, she has had one within the previous year, which is recent enough not to require repeating.

She also advises us that Kathy needs to get her teeth cleaned, and any cavities repaired, along with any other dental work that needs to be done. They want her mouth in perfect condition, since it can be a primary source of infection in someone whose immune system is suppressed, as she will be after the transplant and is taking several anti-rejection medications. This is just one more obstacle in qualifying for a transplant.

July 9 – Kathy receives her pneumonia vaccination, along with a TB test, and tetanus/diphtheria booster. The TB test comes back negative. Another step is taken toward qualifying for a transplant. However, it seems like every time we clear one obstacle for the transplant, another appears. This will continue for the next several weeks.

July 16 – Kathy goes to Dr. B2 to have her teeth cleaned and a general checkup of her mouth and teeth. During this, he finds that Kathy needs an extraction and a root canal in order to make her mouth a healthy as possible, and minimize the risk of infection after her transplant, since a human mouth can be laden with bacteria.

July 20 – A root canal and extraction is performed by Dr. R2 to correct the problems identified by Dr. B2. Dr. R2 sends a letter to Dr. B2 regarding his work.

There is a great sense of urgency at this point, since we're working very hard to get all the tests done as quickly as possible so Kathy can qualify for being listed for a transplant. And, her condition is deteriorating.

She's beginning to have difficulty getting up and down the stairs at our home, and needs a cane for balance and support while walking. She's growing weaker and it's obvious. Eventually she will need a walker to get to and from any room, and will need assistance in simply going to the bathroom at night, which will happen several times in a given night. She spends a lot of time on the couch with little energy to do anything. At one point I stood in the hallway looking at her lying on the couch, almost lifeless. I wept quietly for a moment, and then pulled myself together, going about what I needed to do to help her.

July 27 – Kathy goes to a local clinic for a mammogram and a pap smear. This is yet another test to assure that there are no complicating issues for someone in line for a transplant. Both tests come back negative. She's taken another step in qualifying for a transplant.

July 28 – Kathy gets her hepatitis A and B booster. One more booster is planned for later in the year, but it turns out later that she has sufficient antibodies that she doesn't need that booster.

July 29 – We make another visit to Dr. B2. He writes a cover letter along with Dr. R2's letter, clearing Kathy from a dental standpoint for a transplant, and forwards all this information to the Transplant Center. Another roadblock is cleared.

August 5-6 – Kathy undergoes more testing at the Transplant Center – an echocardiogram of her heart and an ultrasound scan of her carotid arteries to check for any blockages and the risk of a stroke, an X-ray and other tests of her lung function, a CT scan of her abdomen; and perhaps other tests that I simply don't recall.

We meet with the dietician, who advises Kathy to go on a higher protein/calorie diet, that is, to increase her protein intake from 40 grams per day per Dr. S's orders, to 75 grams per day; and from 1,200 calories per day to 1,700 per day. The dietician also advises Kathy to go on a low sodium diet, that is, one with less than 2,000 mg per day. She did not mention any lower limit for sodium. This becomes critical later, since Kathy is also on aldactone, a diuretic for preventing fluid buildup in her body. The combination of taking aldactone and a low sodium diet result in Kathy's blood sodium becoming critically low. We'll come back to that.

Near the end of the visit, we also meet with Dr. E, the surgeon. He takes us through the process of the surgery and tells us about the risks, i.e., dying before you get a donor (10-15%), dying in the first year after a transplant (10-15%), dying within the first next four years after a transplant (10-15%).. I had already read something similar. He notes dryly that "If you survive the first five years, something else besides liver failure is likely to kill you." I also ask him about his use of check lists, hold points, and what amounts to the process control techniques that he uses to assure a good surgical process and outcome. He answers these questions very well, and when asked also states that he's done this type of surgery "hundreds of times." Kathy and I feel reassured. We don't want a surgeon who is new at this.

I later learn about and read an excellent book titled "The Checklist Manifesto" by Dr. Atul Gawande, a surgeon. Among other things it outlines a general surgical checklist developed for the World Health Organization that reduced complications following surgery by 37%, and perhaps more importantly reduced deaths by 47%, worldwide.

These improvements were based on 4,000 patients in eight different countries, and were irrespective of the type of surgery, and whether or not the surgery was performed in a poor country, like Tanzania, or a rich country like the US. Additional details of this checklist are provided in Appendix D. If necessary, you're strongly encouraged to determine whether or not your hospital applies the principles embodied in these checklists.

August 7 – On returning home, we immediately begin increasing Kathy's protein consumption. She has a lot of difficulty eating enough to consume 75 grams per day, but does manage over 60 per day.

August 8 – I take Kathy to the emergency room in the early morning. She has moderate encephalopathy, but it is not as bad as a previous episode. They keep her for a few hours, giving her several saline IV's until her condition improves. Her medications are changed slightly and she is discharged.

August 9 – The day is uneventful. Kathy sleeps most of the day, and eats very little.

August 10 – *Another setback.* In the morning Kathy seems very tired from the night before, and I cannot wake her. I simply think it's from the liver disease and from the episode in the hospital. Around 8am I go to get her new prescription filled at the pharmacy and to the bank. When I get home around 9am, she has severe encephalopathy. She does not know who she is or where she is. She even thinks a closet is a bathroom. With considerable effort I get her into the car and rush her to the hospital.

On the way ask her who I am. She looks at me with a confused, foggy, drunken look, and finally slurs out Ron Moore, and then seconds later slurs out Robert Morris, then Ron Moore again (We joke later that month about who this Robert Morris character is). On arriving at the hospital, blood tests indicate her blood ammonia is 150. They immediately begin saline IV's, and a clear liquid diet. After three days in the hospital, she finally seems well enough to be discharged on August 12. We have no doubt this is from the higher protein consumption ordered by the dietician at the Transplant Center, and so we return to the 40g per day recommended by Dr. S and Kathy's personal dietician. We have no further episodes of encephalopathy after returning to a strict 40 gram per day protein limit. Another lesson is learned.

August 13 – *Another major setback*. We receive a phone call from the Transplant Center that the ultrasound of Kathy's carotid artery has identified a stenosis, or blockage, of greater than 70% in her left carotid artery. This is a really serious setback, since it places Kathy at risk of a stroke, and more importantly, immediately takes her out of consideration for a transplant until it is resolved. More tests are ordered. *We are very discouraged.*

Kathy continues to use a walker to get about, and needs help with nearly everything. Her strength continues to wane, along with her appetite. She forces herself to eat just a little every meal to sustain some level of strength and muscle mass. She works hard to get the 40g of protein per day. Many days it is a struggle. Some days she simply doesn't achieve it.

August 14-25 – Somewhere during this time period, Kathy develops what I call "the death look" This is a look that I noticed in a picture of my father a few months before he was diagnosed with terminal lung cancer, and died two months later. The look is similar to someone with their eyes a bit bulged, and starring into nothingness, as if in a daze. When combined with her lack of appetite, and her need for assistance in doing nearly everything, I am very worried about her. I don't think she has very much time left. We will learn later that my concern is well founded.

Kathy has been too sick to attend mass for several weeks. The last time she went, she had to leave to lie down in the car and wait for me. Because of this, Father Michael comes for a visit to bring Kathy communion, and to give her the sacrament of the sick. Years ago it was called last rites. We hope it will not be her last. Father is very gracious, kind, and spiritual. He lifts our spirits and gives us hope for the future. He leaves us both feeling good.

August 26-28 – We go to the Transplant Center for more testing. Kathy sleeps in the back seat most of the way there, The tests include a follow up test to clarify the stenosis found with the ultrasound of her carotid artery. We're advised that a surgical procedure may be necessary to remove any blockage in her carotid artery before any transplant, and are given information on this. *The anxiety intensifies.* At this point it's obvious that Kathy's condition has deteriorated even further. She can barely walk and needs a wheelchair to go more than a few feet. After doing a pre-treatment because her blood platelet count is so low, the Transplant Center does a CT scan of both carotid arteries, and considering they were concerned about blockages in general, the doctor also orders a chemical stress test of her heart to determine if there are any blockages there as well. After all this, we return home, with Kathy sleeping in the back seat the entire way.

September 2 – It's our anniversary today. We spend it quietly at home wishing each other happy anniversary, hoping we will be able to celebrate it next year.

September 3 – *Good news, at last.* The most recent tests reveal that there is no significant stenosis of her carotid arteries, nor is there any evidence of cardiac ischemia, or restriction of its blood supply. Her heart's myocardial perfusion image (a test of the heart's function) is normal, and she had no infarction, or dead tissue. What a *huge* relief this is, a burden has been lifted from our shoulders. Apparently the ultrasound was not done properly. It appears that the technician put too much pressure on the carotid artery in her neck, constricting it and making it seem like a blockage. This error prompted much anxiety and stress on Kathy, and resulted in unnecessary and risky tests, particularly considering her weakened condition. Perhaps more importantly, it put Kathy's transplant listing at risk, or at the very least of being delayed. Delays can be deadly. It's also one more lesson learned about medical tests.

At long last, Kathy has completed all the tests that are required, and has completed all the vaccinations and other medical procedures. Now we must wait for the transplant team to evaluate all the results and determine if she is qualified for a transplant, and if so, where she is on the list. The wait is nerve wracking, agonizing even. Kathy keeps saying "What will be, will be." I'm not one to accept this view and typically want to take action that will assure the highest probability of the most positive outcome. Unfortunately, she's right. There's little else we can do but wait. While we wait, the regular flu shot becomes available, and so we get our flu shots, but not the H1N1 shot since it's still not available. This continues to be a worry, since an infection like this with her weakened immune system could be fatal.

September 4-9 – We continue to wait. Kathy continues to grow weaker, while my anxiety grows stronger. I'm so scared.

The Listing
and Subsequent Crisis

5

September 10 – Even with a walker or cane, Kathy can barely walk now, and so a wheelchair becomes an everyday requirement anytime she leaves home. She needs help with everything – getting dressed, going to the bathroom, bathing, etc. She has to force herself to eat. She does still feed herself, which is positive. She has great difficulty getting up and down the stairs in our home, and has to stop on the way up, sometimes more than once and catch her breath. She limits her trips up and down to once per day. She naps or sleeps most of every day. I keep the mobile phones with me wherever I go, just in case we receive a call from the Transplant Center.

While Kathy is taking a nap in the late afternoon, and I'm out jogging, the nurse coordinator calls from the Transplant Center and advises us that the team has approved Kathy for a transplant, and that *she is number one on the transplant list* in her blood group with a MELD score of 23. Words are difficult to find that describe my feelings at that moment. After an initial surge of heartfelt relief, I turn to a clinical mode – When do we need to be there? If she's number one on the list do we need to leave tonight? What do we need to do in the short term? Do we need to change her medications at all? And so on. The coordinator indicated that we should come as soon as possible, because the donor could become available at any time, or we could have to wait for weeks. The timing is simply not very predictable.

I run home, literally, and wake Kathy up. As tears swell into my eyes, I tell her she has been approved and is *number one on the list*. She smiles and we hug, a very long hug. It's a huge relief, given Kathy's continuing deterioration, but it's also scary. Like anyone else, we've never been through this, and we know that we're facing major risks and struggles. This path, however, is better than the alternative of certain death.

The coordinator did say that we had to get blood work done locally in order to get an update on her MELD score. The score can vary from week to week, up or down. So, we plan the next day to go to a local hospital where the blood work will be done and then faxed to the Transplant Center. We also begin our plans for packing and moving. I had already put together a checklist for moving – things to do to close the house, people to call, phones to forward, contacting the apartments and selecting one for our move, and a host of other things. It's in Appendix E for those who have an interest.   I call all the immediate family to let them know that Kathy has been approved and we'll be moving in the next day or so to the Transplant Center area. I also send out an email to other friends and family. As times goes by I learn that email will be a more efficient way, vs. phone calls, of letting all our friends and family know what's happening. The email was short and to the point, as I had little time to tarry:

> All –
>
> This is just a brief note to let you know that Kathy has been approved for a liver transplant. She is no. 1 in her blood type group – right now she's at the top of the list.
> We have to go to the hospital tomorrow to have her blood work updated and sent to the transplant center to confirm this, and there may be others who come along who are sicker than she is, but it's not likely. This typically means a transplant is forthcoming within ~2-8 weeks, perhaps sooner.

With this news we will be moving temporarily to the Transplant Center. We'll advise you of our new address, as we will be living near there for the next 3-4 months. You can still reach us on the home/business phone no's, since they will be forwarded to our mobile phones; or you can dial the mobile no's direct. Either works.

We'll keep you posted when we get the call for the actual transplant and her progress thereafter.

Ron

September 11 – *A Crisis Day.* This is a memorable day in US history, and now a memorable day in our history. We arrive at 8am at a local hospital for her blood work, and then return home to begin packing and moving. At 10am we receive a call from the nurse at the Transplant Center who is asking many questions – Is Kathy awake? Is she coherent? How is she functioning? All were frightening questions. Why are you asking? The coordinator advises us that Kathy's blood sodium is critically low at 107, when normal is 135-140. In fact she can't believe it and directs us to return to the hospital for a second test. I call Dr. S urgently to tell him about this. He nearly shouts "What? That couldn't be right? You get that test done over." He is incredulous, scaring me even more. And so, we return to the hospital for another blood test, STAT, or immediately, and then we go home to continue to pack and await another call. The call comes as soon as we get home. It really is done STAT. The results are essentially the same at 108.

The coordinator at the Transplant Center says we need to get Kathy to a hospital NOW, preferably to the Transplant Center. I ask if we have time to get her there without putting her at any additional, substantial risk. The qualified answer is yes, if she can make the trip, they would much rather have her there, rather than treat the problem from there. More critically, she's number one on the list, and needs to be *there*.

After conferring with Dr. S again, we decide to go **now** to the Transplant Center. It's 11am. Packing and getting through my checklist before leaving is a blur. I'm glad I put together the list before hand. I call Liz and let her know what's happening, and ask her to contact the rest of the family.

By 1pm we're on the road to the Transplant Center, and I've organized getting an apartment from our list. I have no idea how it was all done in two hours. I'm sweating profusely as we drive away. Kathy is as comfortable as I can make her in the back seat with pillows, blankets, snacks, books. She's very weak, but responsive. She has no recollection of the two hours and only a little recollection of the morning. On our way to the Transplant Center I call our friends and neighbors Ron and Arlene, and our friends Sue and Lindelle to let them know what is happening. They had already offered to look after the house in our absence.

On arriving at the Transplant Center, Kathy is immediately hospitalized and placed on saline IV's. She may have been given other treatment, but I simply don't recall. We meet with Dr. N and he advises that she is very sick, but he is optimistic that the problem with her blood sodium can be corrected with minimal long term effects. I ask if this will affect her status on the transplant list and he cautiously says it shouldn't. We find out that later that she was temporarily taken off the list until this problem was brought under control.

September 12 – I have little recollection and no notes of what happened on this day. It's simply gone from my memory. Clearly, they continued to treat her critically low sodium, and took her off the aldactone, which along with a low sodium diet put her in this condition in the first place, another lesson learned. I vaguely remember going to the apartment, signing the lease agreement, paying the rent, and dropping off our clothing, and returning to the hospital for the rest of the week.

September 13 – Kathy had been improving, but is now nauseous and weaker. By the afternoon she becomes very ill with nausea and abdominal pain. She's given medication for this, odansetron for nausea and loritab for pain, which provide some relief. She sleeps through the night and is feeling somewhat better in the morning.

September 14 – She seems to be doing slightly better until after a clear liquid supper. After this she has a steady sharp pain in her abdomen, is very nauseas, finally developing dry heaves. After this, she develops a sharp pain in her left arm, shoulder and chest.

She is given more anti-nausea and pain medication, but this provides no relief for the pain in her left arm or chest. The doctors do an EKG, x-rays, and blood work. The results indicate that she has *not* had a heart attack, but the edema or fluid buildup, is increasing and causing swelling and pressure on her heart and lungs. She may be developing congestive heart failure. It's very difficult to maintain an objective view and stay optimistic while the obstacles continue to pile up.

At one point during the night she says "I don't think I'm going to make it." My stomach goes into a knot. I look at her and say in a very firm voice "NO. You're going to make it. I want you to think about Jake and Laura (our two handicapped kids) and tell yourself 'I'm going to make it, for them'." She says OK, but then asks me to promise that if anything happens to her, that I will make sure Jake and Laura are well cared for. I promise. This is the lowest point in our transplant journey. My fear and anxiety peak. I can only hope my words will inspire her to hang on. She is given morphine and finally goes to sleep.

September 15 – She is feeling much better this morning. The saline IV is continuing, but her hemoglobin is very low, requiring a blood transfusion of two units. She also requires an IV of magnesium to help with her electrolytes, and an IV of albumin to help with her kidney function. Her edema, or body fluid buildup continues, and she now weights 159 pounds, compared to the 139 when we arrived, just three days ago. In the evening she continues to have nausea, vomiting, and finally dry heaves through the night without any relief, in spite of the medications that are supposed to minimize these symptoms. She's so sick that these medications just don't work.

I send out the following email to friends and family:

> All –
>
> Just a quick update on Kathy's status as of Sept 15. Last Friday her blood sodium was ~107, confirmed by additional tests, and quite a worry. We drove immediately to the TC, where she's been hospitalized since, taken off aldactone, put on a substantially higher dose of Rifaximin, and been on a saline IV since then. Those should stop today.
> Last night she also had a series of IV's of albumin (~150g total) for her kidneys, and an IV for magnesium to help better control her electrolytes. All this has resulted in an increase in edema, but they're willing to have that to preserve her kidneys and keep the sodium and potassium close to normal.
>
> This increase in edema also resulted in additional pressure on her abdomen, particularly her heart and lungs. Night before last she was in considerable pain in the upper abdomen, particularly with pain up her left arm and left chest. Another EKG confirmed there was no heart attack, but it's believed the increase in edema put pressure on her chest and the resulting pain. An X-ray indicated fluid buildup, but not enough yet to require any physical tapping and draining.

Her blood test also indicated her hemoglobin was quite low at 6 and so last night they did a transfusion of two units, which boosted that up. Her Meld score has also increased to 28, indicating further deterioration of her liver. The good news in all this is that she's at the very top of the transplant list for her blood group, and today she's been feeling a bit better, after considerable nausea all week. Say a little prayer for her when you get a moment...

Thanks for all your help while we're gone.

Ron

September 16 – It's late morning, and having been up all night with nausea and dry heaves, she's finally sleeping. Her weight will peak at 175 with the continuing fluid buildup, 36 pounds more than when she entered the hospital nearly a week earlier. Her MELD score has been updated to 28. Clearly, she's getting worse, even worse than I had imagined. She should receive the next donor liver. We can only hope this will be soon enough. More tests are done on her abdomen to see if there's anything to be concerned about. I don't recall ever being given the results of these tests, but apparently there's nothing remarkable beyond what is already known.

At last, some good news for Kathy. We're informed in the afternoon that she has a donor, a person around 20, who we're guessing is on life support. The doctors advise us that she should have the surgery tomorrow morning and that the liver of this donor is "perfect". Every prospective transplant patient is given medical information on the medical condition of the donor liver, and is given the right to refuse any donor. Most don't refuse. We did not.

I say a prayer for the family of the donor, asking God to comfort them in their grief, asking that the donor be held in God' arms, and thanking God for this gift of life for Kathy. It is a strange feeling, knowing that someone has died to save your loved one's life, and yet to be so grateful that your loved one will live.

The Transplant Surgery 6

September 17 – Sleep was difficult last night. We wake up early and very anxious, nervous, but eager to get on with the transplant. Then we wait, and wait. While no one has said so, apparently there have been delays in "harvesting" the organs of the donor and getting all the paper work done. While the word is often used, "harvesting" seems like such a callous word. I haven't come up with a better one, but maybe even getting, or providing, or collecting, or something, anything, that shows more respect for the dignity of the donor and family would be appropriate. The anxious waiting continues.

Kathy is finally brought into the prep area around 6pm. She sees the anesthesiologist and one of the surgical nurses. Liz and Charlie have rushed to join us once we received the word that Kathy had a donor. While going through the preliminary prep work, Kathy asks Charlie to say a little prayer. He does an eloquent job. Besides being a nurse, Charlie is a former pastor, and has a wonderful way with words. They're comforting and encouraging.

Before they take Kathy into surgery, the nurse advises us that they will call us in the waiting room every couple hours to let us know the status of the surgery. This is reassuring. They come to take her into surgery at 6:45pm. I kiss her and tell her I love her just before they wheel her off. I watch her disappear as they take her into the operating room. It is very difficult not to cry. Charlie, Liz and I all hug.

Now, we wait…and wait. It's agonizing, boring, tedious, worrisome, frightening. After two hours I'm expecting a call from the OR, but none came. The tension mounts as the time passes. Finally, after about five hours, we receive a call from the OR, and the nurse says she's doing fine. It's a quick, even curt call. She's doesn't seem interested in answering any questions, or dallying. My impression, being a bit of a worry-wart, is that things are more difficult than usual, and she really wants to get back to the task at hand. I thank her, and we continue to wait.

September 18 – The waiting continues until 3am. Finally, Dr. E, the surgeon comes in and tells us that the surgery went well, but that he had some difficulty getting the old liver out. Because of this he advises that he may have to go back in and do some "clean up." So, we shouldn't be overly concerned if this happens. While this is said to prepare us, and not alarm us, it adds more worry to my state of mind. He says her liver was about the size of a grapefruit or large orange, and my impression is that it was "stuck" to the other organs, requiring extreme care in its extraction. He had told us when we first met him that the most difficult part of the surgery was getting the old liver out. Certainly that's been true in Kathy's case. Dr. E does at one point smile and say that having done several hundred liver transplants, that if he ever had to have a liver transplant, Kathy is getting the one he would want. This is encouraging. I think of the donor family. I hope they can take some comfort in knowing that their sacrifice has made it possible for others, and Kathy in particular, to live. After he gives us the briefing, I remark to Dr. E that I didn't think Kathy had more than a month or so left to live. He responds "I don't know how you knew that, but you're right." I simply knew.

Reflecting on Kathy's MELD score, and its use in setting priorities for transplant patients, I suppose it is the best available tool to set those priorities, but I wonder if it could be improved. Kathy's MELD score a month earlier was 23, then it went to 20, then just before the surgery it was 28, all in the course of a month. I understand medical data for an individual can vary, since the body is a very complex system, and the testing instruments and systems for collecting the data also have inherent variability. But, a question that comes to mind is: Should the values of the numbers used to calculate the MELD score be pegged at each one's maximum at any given time?

Clearly with end-stage liver disease the person is not going to get any better, and a variation of the number could simply be a variation in the testing procedure, or in the individual based on any number of factors. Taking the maximum value seems a better approach because of this, particularly in light of the need to minimize the risk of the patient's death before the transplant. Alternatively, perhaps there are maximums in each category used to calculate the MELD score for which you might give "bonus points", because if that function is severely limited, then it doesn't matter if the other functions are better, since the person will soon die from that dysfunction. There are likely many other debates and discussions that could be had on this topic, and I'll have to leave it to others to address those. I simply believe the MELD score could be improved upon as a means for determining liver transplant priorities.

After the surgery, Kathy is transferred to the Intensive Care Unit (ICU) and we go to see her around 4:30am. We've already been told she will have any number of tubes and wires coming from her body, and she will be on a ventilator to help her breathe. As promised, this is all true.

The most obvious thing is the ventilator, but there are any number of other "lines" – an arterial line, a central line in her neck, IV's for saline, insulin, albumin, pain killers, sedatives, and perhaps other medications, a so-called swan to monitor her heart and lung function, a catheter for obvious reasons, a so-called JP port in her abdomen to drain fluid from the massive trauma from the surgery, and perhaps other tubes were protruding from her body. It's hard to remember them all.

She seems to recognize us, though today she remembers little of this period. In spite of all the stuff coming from her body, she looks great. Yes, these things are scary and intimidating. But she's alive, and her color is pink. Pink! She's been a yellowish brown for months, and now she's pink! It's wonderful. Charlie and Liz are with me, and we are all in tears at the sight of her, hopeful, happy tears. We encourage her about how well the surgery went, telling her that the doctor said she has an excellent liver and did really well during the surgery. In moments of consciousness, she nods and even tries to smile when we could talk with her. Clearly she is in a lot of pain and discomfort, but she is very courageous.

Charlie's specialty is working in ICU, and all this is familiar to him. He and Liz are both pleased with the competency of the ICU staff, and give them excellent "marks" for their performance. It's all encouraging. We go back to the apartment for a couple hours sleep and a shower.

I send an email to friends and family:

All

As many of you know, things have moved very rapidly the past few days, reflecting the seriousness of Kathy's liver disease. Her transplant surgery was a success, completed this morning at 3am with a "perfect" liver according to the surgeon.

We're very grateful to the family of the donor for giving the Kathy the gift of life. She is in ICU and recovering very well with some expected bleeding from the surgery that may require additional work, but at this point we're very encouraged by the results, and by her courage and determination. Given the size and condition of her old liver (a large cirrhotic orange), the doctors were amazed she could even function at all before the surgery.

Thank you all so very much for your thoughts, prayers and encouragement. They are deeply appreciated (but please don't stop just yet). My best to all.

Ron

Sept 19 – Kathy continues to do well in the ICU. She's now more conscious and able to respond to our questions with nods and shakes of her head. She's still on a ventilator, but they are now trying to wean her from it, by removing it from time to time to see how well she can breathe on her own, and how well she maintains her oxygenation level. She's doing well. During one of these weaning periods, she coughs up a huge blood clot, which without exaggeration was about the size of a baseball. I wonder how she could breathe at all with that in her throat. It must have been a huge relief to get that out. Now she can breathe much better.

Around this time, one of the ICU nurses brings me a device to help Kathy learn to breathe on her own again. Essentially she is to breathe through the device by taking in long steady breaths, trying to hold a small ball between two marks in the device for at least 10 seconds. The nurse tells me to have her do this "10 times per hour, 10times." So, I repeat those instructions back to the nurse "10 times per hour, 10 times." She says "Yes!"

So, being the pedantic, rule-bound person that I am, I do a quick calculation and determine that this is every six minutes, 10 times, for 10 seconds. While that hardly seems enough time to rest between sessions, I proceed. The first couple of times Kathy does pretty well with this exercise, but around the third time she seems "winded" and is unable to complete the exercise. I go to the nurse and tell her that Kathy is having difficulty doing the exercise and ask if this is a problem or if we should be worried. She indicates it could be, and as I'm explaining what we've been doing, she says "No, no!" "No what?", I respond. She says, "You're not supposed to have her do the deep breathing 10 times with each exercise, rather only one time with each exercise, 10 times per hour. But you said "10 times an hour, 10 times." She responds that she was only emphasizing the need to do it 10 times an hour. "Oh," I limply reply. After this, we do the exercise 10 times per hour, one deep breath per time. Kathy's breathing and ability to do the exercise are much better after that. We now laugh about this and how simple instructions can be so poorly interpreted.

Sept 20 – Kathy is off the ventilator and breathing on her own, is cogent and functioning well enough to be transferred to the 10th floor, a "step-down" unit for transplant patients. That day she tells us about the "dark nurses" she encountered one of the nights she spent in the ICU. Recall that she was heavily sedated and on a ventilator, so she couldn't talk; the room was dark, so she couldn't see them very well (hence the "dark" characterization), but she desperately wanted them to get me. Being on a ventilator, she couldn't ask for this. She was crying, and felt so very, very helpless. She described it as one of the worst nights of her life with intense feelings of helplessness and abandonment, one of total despair. Her story made me very sad. All I could do was say "I'm sorry."

About this time Julia, another of Kathy's sisters, arrives to help with her care. When Kathy first suggested this, being the independent, self-reliant person I am, I said "No, I'll be all right." But in her wisdom, even in her reduced mental and physical state, she insisted. Boy am I glad! At this point I'm very tired, and Charlie and Liz have gone home. So, having Julia around to help is a godsend. We begin alternating nights of staying with Kathy in her hospital room, sleeping in a small chair bed, if and when we're not helping Kathy with whatever her needs are, e.g., going to the toilet, needing medication, needing a nurse, or simply needing to be comforted. Every time Kathy moves in the bed, or makes any noise at all, I wake up. It's the same with Julia.

So, there's not much sleeping on the night's Julia and I are on duty to help her. It is good, however, to have every other night available for a good night's sleep. And, during the time when she wasn't with Kathy, Julia is setting up housekeeping by shopping for groceries and household supplies, and generally making our apartment actually livable. You may recall that when we arrived, I only had time to pay the first month's rent, hang our clothing in the apartment, and little else, and then go to the hospital to be with Kathy. I haven't been back to the apartment since.

September 21-24 – Kathy's progress continues. She is able to sit up in a chair, to get to the toilet with help, bathe with help, and walk a short distance, again with help. On her first walk with the therapist, she shuffles, an old woman shuffle, hesitant, pausing. I walk behind her with a chair, just in case she needs to sit. But, she's walking. She seems to be tolerating her medications well, although she has substantial trembling in her hands. So much so, that she needs help eating and with other routine functions. She can drink through a straw, but must hold the cup with both hands. Julia and I are brushing her teeth.

We're advised by the hospital staff that this trembling should diminish with time as her body gets accustomed to the medications.

Somewhere during this time, I do a really dumb thing. As you know, Julia and I are alternating nights staying with Kathy, and at this point, I'm really tired, not just from the past week, but also from the months of helping Kathy day-in and day-out. So one evening when Julia is on duty with Kathy, I decide that I want to get a really good night's sleep. My habit is to read a book while sipping on a glass of wine at bedtime, lulling myself to sleep. But this night I want to *really* make sure I sleep, so I take a sleeping pill as well before an early bedtime.

Big mistake! It ranks right up there with taking a laxative and a sleeping pill on the same night. It's a painful lesson. I don't remember going to sleep, reading the book, or even sipping the wine. I do remember waking up in the middle of night with red wine all over the bed of white sheets, white pillow cases, cover and skirt, and all over my white pajamas, and the beige carpet.

At that point I figure the damage is already done, so I just go back to sleep, thinking as I drift off "I'll take care of this in the morning." Of course, in the morning I strip the bed, and myself, and clean up as best I can. Fortunately for me, Julia saves the day by going on line that afternoon and finding that equal parts of Dawn^{tm} and hydrogen peroxide rubbed into the stain, let soak, and then washed, will take out this stain. It did. I wouldn't recommend the experience to prove the technique. Julia continues to be a huge help in caring for Kathy, and me now, in my dumbness.

September 25 – Kathy is well enough to be discharged on this beautiful fall afternoon. We are very encouraged. We were told in the beginning that a typical stay after the surgery is two weeks, and it's only been one week. They actually considered discharging her the day before, but couldn't get the paper work done in time.

While optimistic, we're also a little scared. We are now responsible for her day-to-day care, not the nurses. It's frightening knowing how critical it is to follow all the instructions on medications, rehabilitation, diet, etc., and there are so many. We are given a "Gray Book" to read before discharge with instructions on what to do; *and* we're given a test before the actual discharge to make sure we understand the instructions. This is an excellent idea. Julia and I both offer our comments on a few inconsistencies in the Gray Book. These are relatively minor, but any inconsistency should be addressed to minimize any confusion in an already difficult process for recovery.

The pharmacist also stops by with all Kathy's medications prior to discharge, and gives us an excellent briefing on each medication, the dose, its purpose, and the timing of the dose. He provides a daily medication log sheet for us to use in keeping track of her medications to make sure we're doing the right medication, in the right dose, at the right time.

One of the instructions that must be followed is continuing to measure glucose or blood sugar before each meal, and at bedtime, or four times per day; and to measure blood pressure and pulse in the morning and at night. A sample vitals checklist is provided in Appendix F, which is abbreviated, since we now only track blood pressure and temperature, along with an occasional check of glucose and weight.

A more comprehensive one would include measuring glucose more frequently. The reason for checking glucose frequently after a transplant is that some 15-20% of transplant patients develop diabetes after surgery, and many experience high blood pressure, both of which must be managed.

Moreover, as time goes by the anti-rejection medications, along with age, weight, and exercise (or lack thereof), increase the risk of diabetes. Another complicating issue is that prednisone typically increases one's appetite, further exacerbating the risk of excess weight and diabetes. During her hospitalization, she required the occasional unit or two of insulin using the criteria that if glucose is between 100 and 125, one unit of insulin is given; between 125 and 150, two units; between 150 and 175, three units; and so on. These are low doses of insulin. Fortunately for us, Kathy has not had any serious problems with either so far, since she's been fairly disciplined about managing these factors.

The dietician meets with us and recommends that Kathy begin immediately with a heart healthy diet, basically the same as was recommended in August, 60-75 grams of protein and 1,700 calories per day. On the other hand, Dr. R, her hepatologist, says that short-term she should eat anything she likes, no matter the nutritional value or lack thereof, just to get some protein and calories into her, including whatever fat that comes with it.
As we'll see, the dietician's recommendations were *not at all* realistic for Kathy for the first few months. Most days she is nauseous; some days she can barely get the minimum of 40 grams of protein that is recommended. She will eventually achieve what the dietician recommended, but that will take several months.

As part of the discharge, they also increase the dose of her primary anti-rejection medication, tacrolimus, by more than 50%. Apparently this is necessary to get the level of the medication in her blood up to within a range that is considered therapeutic or effective. That is, at that level the risk of rejection is much less.

That afternoon in our apartment she is coughing up clear sputum, and has difficulty speaking, being only able to whisper. I contact the Transplant Center and advise them of this, but it is apparently not serious enough to have her return. Over the weekend, initially Kathy seems to do fine, but as the weekend progresses, she becomes weaker, and has a poor appetite. The trembling in her hands and arms intensifies, particularly when she has to exert herself any at all. In her weakened state almost everything is an exertion. For example, when getting into and out of bed to go to the toilet, her arms literally flail. When this happens, I hold her and comfort her. The trembling has reached the point of being scary. When sitting, she is generally disengaged, staring into space in a trance-like state. She responds to questions with "OK," or "Fine" when we ask, while smiling weakly.

September 27 - Sunday, she asks us several times to make sure we do not miss her appointment on Monday. It was almost obsessive. What runs through my mind is "Does she sense something is wrong?"

September 28 – On Monday morning at 3am, I think she had a mini-seizure. When helping her get her back into bed after going to the toilet, her trembling, already pretty bad, becomes "wild", that is, she is shaking wildly and her arms are flailing in the air. She finally collapses onto the bed and her eyes glaze over for a few seconds. She comes out of this, and I ask "Are you OK?" She responds simply "Yes." I tuck her in and she goes to sleep. I'm worried, very worried.

On our way to her appointment at 9 a.m. that morning with the nurse coordinator we bump into Dr. E and mention that Kathy's trembling is worse. He indicates that this is fairly common and nothing to worry about.

We meet with the nurse coordinator, and I observe that Kathy's trembling is much worse, and that she seems more disengaged. After describing what happened around 3am that morning, I ask whether Kathy may have had a mini-seizure. She shook violently, and then went blank for a few seconds. She says no, that trembling is normal. I also ask if she might need a handicap sticker for parking, but she says no, just keep walking and things will be fine. It all seems so scripted, and even dismissive. I'm still worried.

The Seizure

7

September 28 – My concerns are well founded. At 2 pm, Kathy has a grand mal seizure, while Julia and I are helping her get out of the shower. It began with trembling which quickly intensified and turned to flailing, and then a complete seizure. Fluids are coming from all orifices, while the shaking continues, though less intensely. The seizure probably only lasts two or three minutes, but it seems like forever, as she shakes and moans. Julia and I just hold her until the seizure ends and she finally becomes limp. I'm thinking "Dear God why is this happening?" Julia keeps saying "It's going to be all right." This is a very frightening moment for us. We work together to get Kathy into a more comfortable position, get things cleaned up, and get her dressed. This is very difficult because she is simply dead weight, as limp as a wet rag. As all this is going on, I call the Transplant Center, telling them what has happened, and of course they say bring her in. We call an ambulance and are at the hospital by 2:30. On the way into the emergency room with Kathy, she remarks cautiously, with a sense of fear in her voice, "This isn't good is it?" I reply "No, it's not, but we'll get through this, one day at a time."

No doubt the Transplant Center nurse coordinator is having second thoughts about my question regarding Kathy having had a mini-seizure that morning. The doctors quickly conclude that the anti-rejection medication, tacrolimus, is responsible for her seizure. While it is reported as a more powerful tool to minimize the risk of rejection, it also apparently has a greater risk of inducing this serious side effect. They suspend the tacrolimus, and then consider putting her on a different anti-rejection medication.

When Kathy gets to her hospital room, the Physicians Assistance, or PA, does some preliminary tests – 1) stick out your tongue and check for any drooping to one side; 2) raise both arms and they should be at the same height; and 3) say Peter Piper picked a peck of pickled peppers. Kathy does these without any trouble, so it does not appear that she has had a stroke, or has any severe brain damage. I recall that I had done these very same tests when Kathy had the hypoglycemic episode in Huntsville so many months ago.

September 28-29 – Monday evening and Tuesday are very long days. We deal with Kathy's incontinence, inability to get out of bed, lack of appetite, and general malaise. This was especially true the night of the 28th. On Tuesday, she is a little better. She walks a few feet, goes to the toilet with considerable help, and eats a tiny bit. The doctors decide to put her on cyclosporine, an alternative anti-seizure medication, and to add a blood pressure medication as a precaution, since cyclosporine can increase blood pressure to an unacceptable level.

A magnetic resonance image (MRI) indicates several brain abnormalities, including two small hemorrhages and significant brain stem swelling. Their initial opinion, which did not change later, is that the tacrolimus caused the seizure and hemorrhages, and that the corrective action taken to correct the very low blood sodium when she was admitted on September 11th caused the brain stem swelling. Apparently her blood sodium level had become very low over a period of time, likely from treating the edema with aldactone combined with the low sodium diet which was providing her <1,000 mg per day. When the sodium level was suddenly increased using saline IV's, swelling of the brain stem was induced.

I ask Dr. N if this swelling would resolve itself over time, allowing her to return to normal. He indicates that it will likely take several months to completely resolve. He also indicates that for a small percentage of patients it does not resolve, and when combined with the other problems being faced, that the patient can end up in a nursing home. Nausea swells into my stomach. Depression threatens. It's another low point in our journey. While he does not provide statistics, I take a "small percentage" to mean about 5-10%. Yes, it's small, but it's still scary. I also ask him about Kathy's chronic coughing, also listed as a side effect of the tacrolimus, and whether the coughing could be caused by the brain stem swelling? He says that the coughing is not likely being caused by the brain stem swelling.

September 29 – Kathy is improving, but an Electroencephalogram (EEG) this morning indicates that she has "slow brain function". Everything is there, but it's slow getting out. These should resolve as the tacrolimus dissipates from her body, and/or as her brain adjusts to a normal level of sodium. The tacrolimus could be causing both problems, but more likely it's a combination of the two. The tacrolimus is expected to dissipate within 48-72 hours with the brain adapting a few days thereafter.

The brain stem swelling from the sodium imbalance is a different issue. It can take a few months before the brain adapts to the normal level of sodium, and the brain stem swelling is gone. This continues to be a worry. I send an email to friends and family:

> All -
>
> A bit of bad news. Kathy was re-admitted to the hospital on Monday, after a seizure Monday afternoon that was induced by one of the anti-rejection medications. Obviously, we're disappointed with this.

They've taken her off the old medication and put her on a new one, but the old one will take a few days to get out of her system and adapt to the new one. She also suffered from very low blood sodium prior to the admission and now that her sodium is back to normal, her brain/neuro system will need time to adapt to the actual "normal" level. She's adjusting and adapting to all of that.

The good news is that both the meds and the low sodium don't appear to have caused any permanent damage to her brain/neuro systems. We hope to be back out of the hospital in the next few days, perhaps going to an intensive rehab facility first, before we go "home" to our apartment here for continued adaptation to the meds and rehab to a normal life. As I mentioned, she has an excellent liver which is functioning nicely (in fact if her only problem was the liver, we wouldn't be here). We'll be working really hard to make sure we get back on track to her good health.

Please continue keep her (and the donor and their family) in your thoughts and prayers, since organ rejection can happen at any time, particularly during the first 3-6 months. Thank you all so very much for your support. It's been such a blessing.

Ron and Kathy

September 30 – October 1 – Kathy continues to improve. While her hands are still trembling, they are much less so. She's holding her own can of Glucerna™, successfully drinking it through a straw with little or no help. Incidentally, Glucerna becomes Kathy's primary food source in the coming months. As we've observed, she has little or no appetite, but needs proper nutrition for helping in the recovery. Glucerna is a nutritional supplement that's specifically designed for people that have, or are at risk of, diabetes. As we've noted, diabetes is a common consequence in some 15-20% of transplant recipients.

She's also put on citalopram, an antidepressant, on October 1st. Dr. R and Dr. E think it will help with her seeming to be depressed most of the time, and it has very few risky side effects, particularly now that she has a new liver and can process the medication.

But, the neurologist, Dr. S2, thinks it's not necessary. So, if the neurologist thinks it's not necessary, why do it? I want Kathy to have whatever is needed, but not have what isn't needed. Julia and I both make this point to her doctors. Sometimes there is no clear decision to be made, even for doctors.

During this week we also receive two consecutive letters, the first stating that Kathy has been taken off the transplant list because of the low blood sodium problem. My response to this letter is "Well, you can't have it back." The second puts her back on the list. My response doesn't change. Some times the paperwork just doesn't keep up with the actual events as they occur. It would seem to be a good idea, however, if the nurse coordinator actually coordinated more closely with the doctors, so that events like this don't occur.

October 2 – It's Friday. Unfortunately, Kathy's trembling is getting much worse, and she seems weaker. Surprisingly, the doctors begin talking about her being discharged to the rehabilitation hospital, but a private room is not available. They do not want her in a room with another patient because of the immuno-suppression medications and risk of infection. We'll need to wait until Monday to transfer her. When asked, they state that the final diagnosis of her liver failure is auto-immune hepatitis. One odd thing happens this night – about 8:30pm while she is sleeping, she holds her hand and forearm vertically in a straight line into the air for about an hour, and there is no trembling! I wonder why. We'll never know.

October 3 – Kathy slept well last night, after having headache medication (a combination of acetaminophen and propoxyphene napsylate), but this morning she is much worse. She is very confused. She doesn't remember her birthday when asked, saying October of 49, or the current month, saying February. Encephalopathy is rearing its ugly head again.

She points toward the foot of the bed and asks to go up (meaning down). She's incontinent, something that hasn't happened since the night of the seizure. Her eyes seem glassy. The trembling is worse, and her hands and fingers are still tending to curl inward, similar to what happened when she had the seizure. Her voice is stronger in that she's not whispering, but her speech is slurred. Her transfer to the rehabilitation hospital is postponed *indefinitely*. She does however perk up when her brother-in-law and Julia's husband, Greg, arrives to visit. Her mental state improves substantially.

October 4 – Kathy continues to be confused. While her appetite seems better and her voice is stronger, her very mild facial paralysis on the left side from the removal of a brain tumor, called an acoustic neuroma, several years ago seems more pronounced, and has for the past few days.

Dr. H does not think the more pronounced facial paralysis is being influenced by the surgery or medications. I did not directly disagree with him, but think her tiredness from all the trauma of the liver disease, the surgery and then the seizure is making her very tired, which makes the mild paralysis on her left side more pronounced. Even when she was healthy, when she grew tired, I would notice a slight increase in this facial paralysis.

She eats well in the morning – Glucerna and half a banana and bowl of cereal. But, then shortly after eating, she vomits, and becomes even more confused. So, we go through the routine of asking simple questions. She doesn't know her birth date, saying September. She did remember me and all our children's names. She finally remembers her birthday, but only after I remind her. She also has aphasia. She says she's not comfortable, saying she is "too stool". After a couple questions, we find that she is too hot.

She grows weaker through the day. She is unable to walk, even though she indicated she wanted to walk earlier. Lunch consists of most of a can of Glucerna. She sleeps most of the day. She also has another IV of magnesium today. While on rounds, Dr. H says she is getting better. I challenge him "If she's getting better, why does she seem so much worse?" Maybe he is only thinking of her liver function and post-op physical recovery, or simply trying to make us feel better. I don't think she's getting better at all.

October 5 – Kathy continues to be disoriented. This morning when asked "Where are you?", she says "Paris." Julia and I later observe that if you going to be somewhere, Paris is a great choice, and much better than being in a hospital. It's a little dark humor between two people who love Kathy very much. We ask the doctors about the hemorrhage on either side of her brain, and are reassured that this will resolve with time.

Her sodium is also low again, and the PA advises us to eliminate all water, but not her liquid food, just water. Kathy walks a few steps before lunch and does some very light exercises with the physical therapist. Kathy tries to tell me she has to go to the toilet, but I can't understand her, until it's too late. We clean things up. I feel at fault for not being more attuned to her needs.

In the afternoon, the confusion continues, and she is very tired. She doesn't know her birthday, the month, or even where she is. The speech therapist asks her a few questions with no luck on getting the correct response. When were you born? "October". Where are you now? "09", and so on. Her answers are often nonsensical. She continues to know me, and our children, but when shown a picture of our grandchildren, she can't recall their names. She calls me Dad in a picture of the two of us.

I ask the PA if it's ok for her to sleep so much. All she wants to do is sleep. The PA will put this in her chart and advise the doctors. I give Kathy a leg rub, as I now do on a daily basis, sometimes several times in a day, to help minimize the risk of blood clots developing there and to help a bit with muscle tone. They also put support hose on her and inflatable "boots" on her legs. These boots inflate and deflate every few minutes to help minimize the risk of clots developing.

Her cyclosporine is reduced to 125mg per dose, twice per day, down from 200mg per day just a few days ago on Friday. The doctors are concerned that she is not adapting to the cyclosporine very well, and hope that the reduced dose will eliminate the encephalopathy. Yet, a reduced dose also increases the risk of rejection. They begin discussing putting her on a third anti-rejection medication. This is very worrisome. We keep being told that she's getting better, but she seems worse every day. Her weight is now 132, down 43 pounds from its peak of 175 just after the surgery, some 17 days ago, when the swelling from the edema was at its maximum. Her weight will eventually bottom out at 122, or 53 pounds less than its maximum.

October 6 – It is very difficult to awaken Kathy this morning. She slept right through the blood draw, needle stick and all, and through a bed change in the early morning, needed because of incontinence. She seems to want to sleep all the time. Her trembling continues to be very bad, and she can barely stand. She continues to be disoriented and has bad aphasia – she mumbles jibberish.

She's knows me, and her birth date, but when asked where she is, she repeats her birth date, several times. When asked about doing a new MRI/Brain Scan, Dr. H seems reluctant to order a new one, indicating that in the past they were more confusing than informative.

By afternoon, she seems to be doing somewhat better, though the confusion continues along with the aphasia. She walks about 100 feet, has a sponge bath, and generally does a bit better. She takes a long nap, and after a deep sleep is totally confused. "Out of it" might be a phrase to characterize her condition. Dr. S2 comes to interview her again, and sees a greater degree of confusion than his visit on Friday, October 2nd. He indicates that the swelling of the brain stem and the tiny hemorrhages should not be causing this, and suggests that the second anti-rejection medication, cyclosporine, may be causing the increased encephalopathy and aphasia.

I'm very discouraged, maybe even depressed. At one point we get Kathy into a chair and as I'm sitting on her bed facing her, I'm hanging my head staring at the floor. Sensing my mood, Kathy gently and clearly says to me "Don't be discouraged," and puts her hand on my shoulder. She's still here! This is the most heartening thing she has said in days. She's very present to me at that moment. We're going to get through this. I give her a long hug.

Later Dr. S2 stops by and Kathy does poorly on his routine test of cognition, asking her things like saying the days of the week backward. After he's finished, I get up in Kathy's face and look deeply into her eyes and ask her "What am I saying?" She says "I love you". My eyes become quite watery. I tell Dr. S2 that she's in there, just having trouble getting out. He agrees. He orders another MRI to compare with the last time. In the afternoon after Julia takes over, she is a bit better. When I call from the apartment, she tells me she loves me and seems much more "connected".

Today we receive cards from Sue and Lindelle, and from our friend Kay, who included a very nice gift certificate from a book store. We'll go book shopping when Kathy's better! I bring the cards to the hospital for Kathy to see.

As Julia reads their card aloud, we all weep quietly, Julia, Kathy and me. The card's hand-written note says "Kathy – I'm sure you felt like you were falling out of a tree these past few weeks and months. Lindelle and I are so proud of your tenacity. Your strength when you don't think you have it in you to move and keep moving, your courage to face unbelievable obstacles and leap over them. I know Ron is being your rock to lean on and that is so awesome. Love is so encompassing! Take care of yourself." How wonderful it is to have such good friends.

October 7 – Kathy is more "connected" this morning, talking more, and making more sense. She still slurs her words a bit (like listening to a child that's learning to talk and having to interpret based on your understanding of the child's abilities). Dr. H2, a young surgeon, stops by, and Julia and I brief him on her improvement.

Dr. H and the transplant team later confirm that the MRI indicates her brain is slightly more swollen, consistent with a toxic reaction to the second anti-rejection medication, cyclosporine. Their conclusion is that Kathy is not tolerating it very well, and this could be due to the fact that it is part of the same family of drugs as tacrolimus that caused the seizure. Dr. S2 had hinted at this yesterday, suggesting that they may have to switch medications yet again. Before doing that however, they've decided to reduce her dose again and see if her symptoms of trembling, encephalopathy, and aphasia are reduced, and whether she can simultaneously maintain a therapeutic level in her blood for anti-rejection. If that doesn't work, they're going to switch to yet another medication. Reducing the level of the anti-rejection medication increases the risk of rejection, so we are both very nervous about this. But, a life of debilitation is not really a quality life.

In the afternoon, Kathy walks a hundred feet or so, and does some exercises and isometrics with her arms and legs, holding her arms horizontal to the side and front, waving, lifting her legs while seated (as if walking), pressing a pillow between her legs, pressing her legs outward while I'm holding them. Then we do some mental and speech therapy exercises, like counting to 50 (we'd only gotten to 20 up until now), her location - town and facility; articulating words like Al-a-bam-a, Mass-a-chu-setts, and so on. She wants to go to sleep at the beginning, but I insist on her sitting in a chair and doing these things. At Julia's suggestion, I tell her that the meds have created little gremlins in her brain and while she's sleeping, they build large walls that stop her brain from getting its messages through, so we can't sleep too long or too hard before the gremlins build the walls too large. I promised that after 30 minutes I'll let her take a nap. At the end of the exercises, which last ~35 minutes, I repeat my promise and ask if she knows how long it's been. She replies "Longer" (than 30 minutes). We both laugh. She's still in there!

Later, while we're with Julia, Kathy makes a funny comment, and then says "Oh no, I'm getting just like my mother." She begins laughing, and so do we. It's a wonderful moment. Another bright spot in our day comes when she receives flowers from our friends Tim and Mary.

She sleeps VERY soundly that night , sleeping right through incontinence and then through the bed changing, even though this occurs in place, rolling her back and forth to change her sheets and blankets and even her nightie. That's very sound sleeping.

October 8 – In spite of the very sound sleeping, she seems to be more connected, even though she is still only about 30% of her normal self. At one point Kathy says the trembling is less, though it's hard for me to see the difference. It seems like a good sign. Dr. S2 comes for an early morning visit, and to test her mental abilities. She doesn't seem to do as well as yesterday's visit. She still can't do things like say the days of the week or the months backward, or even add 8 + 6.

But, her complex thinking seems good. She makes remarks about her father and mother, for example saying that she didn't spend enough time with her Dad. She tells Dr. S2 that she's not doing as well as yesterday, and is tired from the exercise. She knows when she's not doing well, which I think is a good thing. Dr. S2 expresses concern about the continued use of cyclosporine and about her blood pressure, which is somewhat high and may be having a negative effect on her brain. He says he's going to talk to the transplant team about these issues. After he leaves, Kathy says "I didn't do very well on his tests did I?" I say "No, but that will come." I actually find it encouraging that she knows that she's not doing well in these neurological tests. At least she's functioning well enough to know that.

At 9am we're still waiting for breakfast, which is one thing that I found particularly annoying during Kathy's stay in the hospital. For no apparent reason, the meals would come anywhere within a two hour band, i.e., 7-9am, 12-2pm, and 5-7pm, and sometimes even outside these times. Just for consistency in the patient's care, it would have been nice to have them come at least within a half hour band, allowing for better management of time and supplemental activities like bathing and toiletry, physical therapy, and so on. I suppose we should be grateful that this was our biggest complaint.

I send an email out to update friends and family:

> All -
>
> An update – first a re-cap. Kathy had her transplant surgery on Sept 18 and was discharged on Sept 25 with an excellent liver, a remarkably short period post-op, given her entry into the hospital on Sept 11, with extremely low sodium levels and their related complications. Unfortunately on Monday, Sept 28, she had a seizure, a result of the toxicity to her from one of the primary anti-rejection medications, and was re-hospitalized with significant neurological symptoms – the seizure of course, as well as trembling, aphasia (difficulty finding words for speaking), and encephalopathy (confusion). So, they switched her to another medication in the same family. She was making good progress with it, and we were scheduled to go to a rehab hospital on Monday, Oct 5. Unfortunately, over the weekend, she developed similar symptoms/problems as she had with the first medication, likely because it is from the same family of medications. So, the transfer to the rehab facility was postponed.
>
> Since then they've done some tests to confirm that the second medication is in fact the cause of those similar neurological symptoms, and have lowered the dose and taken other steps to adapt her to it, with the hope that it will work after all. This seems to be working and she's making good progress in recovering, but we're still in the trial phase of the new dose and approach.

All these symptoms, we're told, will reverse or resolve as we get the meds right. We should know in the next week or two if it's going to work. I expect they'll be scheduling a new time for her to go to a rehab hospital, probably next week, but that will depend on the progress she makes with the new approach. Once at the rehab facility, we'll be there for ~ one week, before we go "home" to our apartment here for continued adaptation to the meds and rehab to a normal life, as well as the follow up visits to the transplant center. The good news - her new liver continues to function really nicely, with all functions in the normal range. But for the neurological problems induced by the medications, we'd have been home long ago. But, without them, the liver isn't likely to accept its new home. So, we (the doctors and us) are working really hard to get the balance right, and get her back to good health.

Please continue keep her (and the donor and their family) in your thoughts and prayers, since organ rejection can happen at any time, particularly during the first 6 months. Thank you all so very much for your support. It's been a real blessing.

Ron and Kathy

October 9 – Kathy seems much better this morning. She has a breakfast of 12 ounces of protein-supplemented milk, along with a can of Glucerna, and of all things, some grits. We need to push solid food and get her into a normal diet as quickly as we can. We have a long way to go on this. Later when the PA stops by, she complains that the stitches are still in and they were scheduled to be taken out. The PA apologizes, and then Kathy says in a jovial way "Shame on you." That's the Kathy that I know, making fun and teasing. The PA observes that she is doing much better, as do Julia and I.

Kathy's fasting glucose today is 98, a normal number. She continues to avoid the complication of diabetes. In the week or two after surgery her glucose levels were slightly elevated and she received an occasional dose of insulin, typically one or two units. I'm not as worried about this now.

At this point her cyclosporine dose has been reduced again to 75 mg, twice per day. We need to understand this, since there seems to be a lot of risk with this. If we get Kathy's neurological issues resolved through a lower dose, we have a greater risk of rejection. Dr. H says her cyclosporine levels are holding at about 125, and if we can do that on the 75mg dose twice daily, she will probably be just fine, especially with the use of other anti-rejection medications, i.e., micophenolate mofetil and prednisone.

Kathy wants to go home, as we all do, and laments not being able to do so. To take her mind off this, we do some arm strengthening exercises with one pound weights, working on her biceps, deltoids, and triceps, but she's very weak.

As the day wears on Kathy develops a stiff neck and requires an acetaminophen and propoxyphene napsylate for pain. Later, she only walks about half as far as yesterday, which was only about 200 feet, but she does well on some arm and leg isometrics. We walk again later in the afternoon, just a bit farther, and we do more arm and leg isometrics. During this, the occupational therapist (OT) comes in and she does even more work, all related to day-to-day living, like getting dressed and taking a bath.

Dr. S2 stops by and gives her a few more tests. Kathy tells him she is really disappointed she didn't "pass his test" yesterday. She cried about it yesterday. I observe again that her complex social reasoning is really quite good, not withstanding that she couldn't say the months or days of the week backward. During his visit, we mute the TV, as we always do when the doctors come on rounds.

While he is asking Kathy questions, which she does poorly in answering, she notices him glancing at the TV. She looks at me and says firmly "Turn it off." He looks at her and says "You caught me didn't you." She replies "Yes, you need to pay attention." This is both funny and encouraging. Maybe she can't add 8 + 6, but she is on top of the social interaction issues. What a wonderful moment it is. I again observe that her complex social reasoning is pretty good. Dr. S2 agrees.

During this visit, he also asks her how she got from home in Knoxville to the Transplant Center, presumably asking about directions to test her memory and complex thinking. Kathy says "Well, I get in the back seat with my book and pillows, and my husband types the address in his GPS and drives us here." We all have a good laugh at this. Her sense of humor is still good as well.

She's getting about 60-70+ grams of protein a day, mostly from Glucerna and protein-supplemented milk, and about 1,100 calories, but still not much solid food, e.g., three bites of chicken salad for lunch; some grits for breakfast; and not much more.

Following a brief nap after dinner, Kathy seems confused again. She's cries, wanting her sister Liz, and wanting to go home. She says "All I do is lay around." Finally she says "Maybe it would be better if I just died." It's another down moment for Julia and me, who both happen to be with her. Julia and I ask her if she thinks Jake and Laura would like her to die; if she thinks I would, or Julia would. Of course, she says "No" to all these questions. Julia points to all the cards she has received and all the people that are wishing her well and want her to be part of their lives. They are her friends and relatives. Julia and I agree that the prednisone is at work again, inducing these mood swings.

Later that night she begs and cries for "white stuff". After much back and forth, I think this is ointment, and that it's hemorrhoid cream. I help put some on when she goes to the toilet, since her trembling is still pretty bad. After she's back in bed, she asks for it again, and is very frustrated. My offer to repeat the application is not well received. She doesn't seem fully connected, and is frustrated at not being able to describe what she wants. The aphasia continues.

It almost seems like she's having a bad dream and wanting "something". I finally conclude that she wants miconazole, a treatment for vaginal itch. I help her with this. This still doesn't do it, and her frustration, and mine, continue. Finally, after many questions and answers, I guess the correct answer, and after searching all over the hospital for it, get her some baby powder (white stuff!). I help her with a sponge bath, and her baby powder. She's content, and sleeps, finally.

October 10 – Kathy's fasting glucose is 103, and her blood pressure is 114/68 this morning, all good numbers. She continues to improve, but she still has difficulty with simple things, vs. recognizing complex social cues.

For example, she still has difficulty adding 8 + 6, saying the days of the week backward, and saying the months backward. We begin practicing saying the days of the week and months *forward*, in normal order. I think that if she can say them forward easily, then saying them backward should come to her.

Her seizure still appears to cause a "curling" of her fingers, so we practice doing finger extensions and making a fist, and touching each finger to the thumb. She is clearly frustrated by not being able to do these simple things and begins saying the months quietly to herself. I tease her that we're going to re-learn all this. She smiles.

She still has little appetite for solid food, but continues to take Glucerna, protein-supplemented milk, and ordinary milk just fine. She agrees to take one bite of each serving from each meal, just to try to learn to like solid food again.

October 11 – Her fasting glucose is 113, not great, but ok. Before breakfast arrives, which could be anytime in a two hour band, Kathy asks for Rice Crispies and Julia gets them. She eats them, with no help from us. This is the first time this has happened in a long time, since before the surgery. While this may not seem like a big deal, it is a huge deal for Kathy and likely other transplant patients, especially since she has had a seizure. Essentially she is relearning almost everything, including simple things like feeding herself, brushing her teeth, going to the toilet alone, and doing simple math. Things that most of us take for granted. She walks a short distance before they finally bring the hospital breakfast. She has a Glucerna, a bite of French toast, and a few bites of oatmeal. The trembling is dissipating as she eats. Progress.

Dr. H stops by. Kathy's neurological function has improved dramatically with the reduced dose of cyclosporine. Unfortunately, with the reduced dose of cyclosporine her liver function, which had been totally normal, has deteriorated slightly two days in a row, an indication of rejection, according to Dr. H. She may not be able to keep her liver on the reduced dose. So, tomorrow they plan to do a biopsy to determine whether she is in rejection. *It's a frightening moment.*

And, the doctors are considering doing an endoscopy to put a stent in her bile duct to eliminate a biliary stenosis, or blockage of the bile duct. Later we let the family know.

Kathy cries after the Dr. H leaves, and says "I'm scared." I reply that "I'm scared too, but we're going to work our way through this, one day at a time." Later, she comes out of the toilet and says "I'm dying." My stomach leaps into my throat and I have an awful sickening sensation throughout my body. I say "NO." She says "We keep coming across obstacle after obstacle at every turn, and it just doesn't seem to be working. I'm ready to quit." I respond firmly "You're not going to quit. We still have more options and we need to work on those first, and we need to wait for the results of the biopsy, before we make statements like that."

"One day at a time." I remind her again. We say a prayer together, thanking God for the liver, and asking for His grace in helping her live, helping the doctors make the right decisions, and helping us to get through this.

I call Julia and ask her to come back from the apartment for a pep talk with Kathy. Julia repeats essentially what I've said, that we have options and we're going to use all of them. Julia suggests going for a walk, and not dwelling on the negative. We go for a short walk, with Kathy walking the entire hospital floor "loop" of about 200 feet, more than she has walked until now. She then does isometrics of her arms and legs. It's a good workout. Again, this may not seem like much, but it is for many liver transplant patients who can barely sit up or get to the toilet in the first few days after the transplant, and Kathy has had a seizure and brain stem swelling, complicating her recovery considerably. Kathy takes a nap, then we talk briefly and then she walks again, to the nurses' desk and back, or about 100 feet.

I call Dr. H and he says the latest tests indicate that Kathy's new liver has deteriorated some, but that's uncertain. They won't really know until they do the biopsy, and that will determine what action to take, including doing nothing. Until it's done, they're taking preemptive action to minimize the risk of rejection by giving her an intravenous dose of 500mg of prednisone, a very high dose, and then tapering it down.

He notes that this may also require insulin shots, something we've avoided now for several days. They will also increase two of her immunosuppressant drugs, the cyclosporine and micophenolate mofetil . After the biopsy they'll have a better idea of what to do. Options include 1) doing nothing, 2) increasing the cyclosporine dose, 3) moving aggressively with another immunosuppressant medication. *The angst is pervasive in the room.*

We try to put this aside for a moment by having dinner together, with me sitting on the bed facing her sitting in her chair, and helping her eat as needed. I tell her how much I enjoy having dinner with her. Such a simple act provides so much joy, particularly now. She stands to get back in bed, and we hug a long hug. It's a touching moment. It's wonderful to hug her, and life is good among all the worries, if only for a moment.

Later that night Kathy asks for a Sprite or 7up. When I repeat this, asking which one she wants, she says "the other one". After many, frustrating tries, I finally guess that she really wants ginger ale. She is clearly frustrated with this. She blurts out "After all these years and you still don't understand me. Julia does, but you don't." After quickly getting over my hurt feelings, I say "But you said Sprite." We smile together finally, then I give her a hug and tell her it's ok, and that I'll work really hard to get it right in the future.

We had been told that prednisone can induce mood swings. This is a good example of this. When you add the prednisone to a common trait of men taking things quite literally, and not being able to "interpret" what their wives are saying, along with all the other issues at hand, you get situations like this. When it happens, try not to react, but rather respond with kindness and love. I kept reminding myself that Kathy was going through a much more difficult ordeal than I was.

October 12 – Kathy's fasting glucose is 140 after the 500mg mega-dose of prednisone. This is actually pretty good, considering the size of the dose. I'm optimistic that she may be able to avoid developing diabetes. Kathy is scheduled for the biopsy this morning, and is NPO (no food or drink). We go for a short walk of ~100 feet, and do our isometrics. The PA stops by and says her liver numbers haven't really changed since yesterday, but only if there is an indication of rejection will they take further preemptive action. She assures Kathy that she has a good liver and that the problems we're seeing are common, and manageable with one or more of several options.

The PA also indicates that if there's a room available, Kathy will go to the rehab hospital today, which is also encouraging. If they were really concerned about rejection, she would continue with her hospitalization in the transplant unit. Kathy seems reassured with this.

The biopsy is done at 10am. It's interesting that the procedure itself takes about 10 minutes, but the waiting, traveling, and paperwork takes another three hours. Dr. S2 stops by and observes that Kathy's neurological function is improving. He suggests more reading and crossword puzzles, and more of any activity that she enjoys.

We wait for the results of the biopsy. We're very apprehensive. Kathy is also given some diuretic today, to help reduce her potassium level back into the normal range of below 5.4 or so. Julia comes in to take over her shift for looking after Kathy. On arriving at our apartment, I sit for a minute, just to rest. I don't know how long I sat there, but the next thing I know, I'm awakened by my phone ringing with a text message from Julia. The biopsy indicates inflammation, but *not rejection*. It's a huge relief.

I immediately call our children, my brother, and Kathy's sisters, *except* I forget to call Liz. I knew in my mind there was someone else to call, but simply could not think. Fatigue does that to you. Liz calls later and I bring her up to date.

When I call Kathy's room after dinner to tell her "Good Night I Love You", she actually answers the phone, something she has not done until now, a very good sign. We share a brief, affectionate moment and then I talk to Julia about how she's doing. It's all good!

October 13 – Her glucose is 114, so I speculate that the effect of the prednisone is diminishing. Kathy is sitting in her chair when I arrive, another good sign. She has some protein-supplemented milk then a Glucerna, and finally a bite of bacon and eggs. This is encouraging. Maybe her appetite is getting better.

Several of the doctors on the transplant team arrive early, Dr.'s C, H3, H2, and one of the PA's. They advise us that inflammation and rejection are very different, and so we will stay the course for now with the current medications, but Dr. C wants to increase her cyclosporine dose, as long as she tolerates it, and asks us all to be aware of any changes in her neurological condition.

She developed encephalopathy and aphasia with the higher dose in early October, so we're worried that this will happen again. The level of cyclosporine in her blood is currently only 83, and they want it to be at least 125 to minimize the risk of rejection. He plans to go to 100mg, twice per day, vs. the current dose of 50mg in the morning and 75mg at night. This higher dose should bring her into the desired level. As and when she can tolerate it, without any neurological problems, he says he will increase it further.

We're advised that a therapeutic range to minimize the risk of rejection is 100 – 400, a pretty broad band. Our experience so far with Kathy is that the dose required to achieve this is roughly the same number in milligrams as the dose she takes twice a day. So, for example, if Kathy is on a 100mg dose twice per day, her blood level of cyclosporine is typically in the range of 100.

We ask about Kathy possibly being discharged and whether she should go to the rehab hospital, or not. During a previous conversation we thought it would be needed, since she couldn't do things like brush her teeth, hold a cup, or care for her toileting without help, and was very weak. Kathy has now progressed to the point where none of that is true anymore, so we feel confident about taking her home without going through rehab first.

After a brief discussion, the decision is made to go to rehab for a few days as necessary, but if no bed is available tomorrow, then go home. We go for a short walk of about 200 feet on the floor of the hospital, without stopping for a rest. She takes slow steady steps, but is still a little wobbly. Much of the lack of balance is due to the previous surgery for the acoustic neuroma, and the resulting loss of balance and hearing in her left ear. When combined with her current condition, it's no surprise that she is wobbly.

She sits and takes her meds, and does a few arm isometrics. She takes a shower, with me helping some, but not as much as in the past. I wash her hair and back, and help with the rest.

Kathy is doing much better, napping at the moment. Later, she tears up and tells me she loves me and how lucky she is. I respond that I'm the lucky one to have her in my life.

Kathy has a lunch of Glucerna and a bite of everything on the tray. She walks the hospital floor, again about 200 feet, and then does some leg isometrics. She's getting stronger. She then brushes her teeth by herself, steadily and surely. She's also eating and taking her medications on her own. These are significant steps forward,

Dr. K, from the rehab hospital, stops by to evaluate Kathy and her ability, and she seems pleased. We'd rather not go to the rehab hospital, but after talking with Dr. C again, along with Dr. S2, and with Kathy, we conclude that a few days in the rehab hospital would be the best course of action.

She is transferred at 7pm in the evening after taking her increased dose of cyclosporine. They advise us that the rest of the medications will be provided at the rehab hospital, and that tomorrow her cyclosporine will be increased again.

When we arrive at the rehab hospital, I advise the nursing staff that she still needs her evening medications and normally takes those at 8pm. After reminding them twice more, at 10:30pm she finally gets her medications. I am not pleased. Attention to detail and consistency are essential for a transplant patient, and this transition has not been smooth. Kathy is in considerable discomfort during night, complaining of pain in her head, back, abdomen. A fairly strong pain medication seems to help, and she sleeps.

The rehab hospital also has some rules that say, among other things: 1) We are not allowed to use our computer in the room (I ignore this, with no consequence); and 2) Visitors times are limited to certain hours. I ignore this as well, since I'm her caregiver, and there does not seem to be a problem with that. Further, I'm not sure about how many people can be with Kathy during the day – can she have two caregivers (Julia and me) during the day, before visiting hours? Apparently she can, and so we do. Exceptions to the rules are apparently made for transplant patients.

That night I notice that the rehab hospital nurses and nurse's assistants don't have much consideration for their patients on the 11pm to 7am shift. They're quite boisterous and loud. They don't seem to understand that their patients are trying to sleep. We were very near the nurses' station, so that tended to make the lack of consideration even more obvious.

October 14 – Kathy's glucose is 110; BP is 110/65, all good. Our 7:30am appointment starts at 8am. The head therapist interviews Kathy with many questions about the environment where she lives, and her goals on returning home. I give the therapist a brief on Kathy's history, both longer term, for example, the acoustic neuroma history; and short term regarding the past few month's difficulties.

The therapist helps her do a sponge bath, which she does fairly well. Kathy puts on hospital scrubs when finished, and they observe her brushing her teeth. She seems to be doing well, save the tiredness and pain. I notice an oozing from the JP port in her abdomen, and change the band-aid covering it. The doctor will check it later.

The speech therapist arrives and conducts a series of tests, mostly questions related to cognitive capability like birth date, age, length of marriage, and then continues with increasingly complex questions, e.g., which is larger a garbage can or pail; which has more leaves, a tree or a bush, and so on.

She asks Kathy to remember three words – lightbulb, hamburger, sweater. Later when asked about these words, Kathy remembers two relatively easily, then the third with help from me by asking her what food our youngest daughter likes best. Kathy does well, though things are still coming a bit slowly. The therapist advises that sitting up straight and drinking directly from the cup should help reduce the risk of the liquid going into her windpipe and choking her.

When Kathy complains about her vision, she advises us *not* to get new glasses just yet, since it's pretty common for a transplant patient's vision to deteriorate because of the medications. She'll provide a journal for Kathy to help with enhancing her short term memory, along with some speech exercises.

I ask the speech therapist if brain stem swelling can cause chronic coughing, indicating that the transplant team did not think it would. The therapist says that people who have had swollen brain stems often have problems with their throat, with both swallowing and chronic coughing. It's another lesson.

After the speech therapist leaves, I ask Kathy to recall the time that Dr. S2 gave her a condensed version of a similar test, and that when Dr. S2 left, she cried and said "I didn't do very well on his test." She remembers this. This time though, I tell her that in my opinion she has passed a more difficult test *with flying colors*. How far she has come in just a week!

The head nurse comes in later and I talk to her about our current situation:

- A week ago I felt strongly that Kathy needed rehab. Now that the medications are being tolerated better and she's much more capable, that is, her mental and physical capabilities are dramatically improved, I no longer find it necessary.
- I'm happy to have the evaluation, and to benchmark her performance, and to determine if there are things I'm not doing that I could do, or if there are things I can't do that she needs on a continuing basis. Speech therapy seems to be one Kathy would benefit from on an outpatient basis. OT and PT do not. I can do those.
- I'm self-employed, and now have been unemployed for several months, taking care of Kathy. I will be unemployed for several months to come to take care of her. And, we have no drug coverage. I don't want to spend scarce funds on activities that I can, and have, done for her, either in the hospital or at home.
- In light of all this, I'd like to get out before the weekend.

Dr. K comes in later and I talk with her as well about this. She is sympathetic, but also notes that there are medical issues that must be addressed, and that Kathy may need another saline IV to keep her sodium and potassium in line. She talks to Dr. C and he agrees that Kathy can go home on Saturday morning, *if* her lab numbers for blood work, liver and kidney function remain stable, having no deterioration.

Several people come in and out in the first day or two that we're here. It seems to be a revolving door. Coming through are Occupational Therapy, which specializes in helping do things like getting dressed, washing and folding clothing, dishes, and other common household tasks.

Then comes Speech Therapy, which is less about speech and more about cognitive skills, communicating, doing simple tasks like reading a menu, calculating change, and so on; the Head Nurse, who talks over people without really listening or answering questions, so I don't like her; the Social Worker, who is empathetic; a Nurse, who has a sweet personality; a Nurse's assistant who appears to do the job, but not too much more; the Head of Nutrition; a Nutrition Tech, and others. My impression is that their overhead must be huge.

October 15 – Kathy's glucose is 115 and her blood pressure is 110/65, all good numbers. She is very tired and sluggish this morning though. She has difficulty waking and getting up. The occupational therapist (OT) comes in and helps her with a sponge bath, getting dressed, and brushing her teeth. She stands and brushes her teeth alone over the sink, another sign of progress. We discuss briefly with Dr. K shifting her blood pressure medications to the evening, since they can cause drowsiness. She agrees to this.

Kathy has breakfast of a can Glucerna, a cup of skim milk and three bites of French toast. Next, we go to physical therapy (PT). She walks 160 feet, rests, then walks 180 feet, with rests every 40-50 feet; then does a final 40 foot walk to wait for occupational therapy. This is good progress. Then she does leg exercises of in/out flexes, tip-toe flexes, side leg lifts, and leg-lifting while sitting. Then she goes on to occupational therapy again for arm exercises using a bicycle pedal mounted on a table and pumping for 10 minutes, then does 10 arm curls with one pound weights, overhead stretches, along with stretching while she puts rings on a stick. This is a really good workout. She fell asleep while doing some of these, and so takes a much needed, but brief nap before lunch.

Lunch is Glucerna, two bites of cheese sandwich, a sip or two of tea, and a sip of tomato soup. She naps briefly again. I know Kathy is very tired, after years of liver disease, bouts of encephalopathy, critically low sodium, brain swelling and hemorrhages, a liver transplant, a grand mal seizure, and so on. Still she carries on. I ask her to describe all the PT and OT in one word. She says firmly, "Enough!" We have a good laugh. I try to remind myself of how far she has come and not to be frustrated when she refuses to eat, or do an exercise, or is a bit oppositional. Sometimes this is difficult, especially when I want so badly for her to be better. I know the more she does, the better she will be in the future.

In the afternoon, she does more OT, doing things like folding clothes, putting plugs in holes, and putting nuts on bolts to develop her fine motor skills. She does a good job.
Then we have speech therapy. This time it's writing, for example, write your name, address, kids' names, occupation, etc.; then setting up and completing a journal of the activities for the day; then doing some mouth exercises for muscle development and articulation. We decide that we'll be using the daily journal for all our future activities.
An example of this daily journal is shown in Appendix G In the afternoon at 4pm, her BP is 118/72 and temp is 98.3. Pulse is 103, and oxygen saturation is 97. All are good and consistent with her history.

It may seem odd that we are so pleased with Kathy walking 300 or so feet, and doing relatively minor exercises and tasks, like folding clothing, all seeming trivial activities. But her physical state has been so very poor. In my mind, any ability to walk or function is a huge step forward, considering that five weeks ago she was using a wheelchair. As the old saying goes, the journey of 1000 miles begins with the first step. We're taking the first steps on the way back to a normal life.

I send an email to update friends and family:

All -

A quick update. Kathy continues to make progress. The transplant team had a liver biopsy done on Monday, Oct 12th, after some of her liver "numbers" indicated a slight deterioration in performance. They were concerned about a possible rejection episode. Fortunately the results indicated a slight inflammation, something that is common to the liver, even yours and mine. So, following the biopsy result we transferred to the rehab facility on Tuesday evening, Oct 13th.

At this point, unless there's a deterioration in her "numbers", we're expecting to be discharged to go home on Saturday, the 17th. There we'll continue with in-home rehab several days a week and twice weekly blood work and nurse/doctor visits to make sure the liver and other body organs are functioning properly.

Please continue keep her (and the donor/family) in your thoughts and prayers, since organ rejection can happen at any time, particularly during the first 6 months. Thank you all so very much for your support. It continues to be a real blessing.

Ron and Kathy

October 16 – Kathy talked a lot in her sleep last night, saying things like "OK, No, Help me, I'm having a baby, I have a sore back, etc". She slept reasonably well, save the talking in her sleep. Her glucose this morning is 116, and her BP is 101/63, good numbers. She showered this morning standing up, with some assistance. This is also progress.

For breakfast she has a Glucerna and a half cup of milk, but no food. I continue to track this, and to be concerned about her appetite. The doctors increase her cyclosporine to 125mg, twice per day.

Then we walk, a bit farther than yesterday, but only once. She climbs 12 steps, vs. 8 from yesterday, but does 4 more steps in the afternoon. Then she does 15 minutes at 15% torsion on the hand bicycle vs. 10 at 10% yesterday, and then three sets of 10 reps each for one pound weights, working on curls, triceps, anterior deltoids, lateral deltoids, shoulder presses. This is a really good workout for her. She's tuckered out now though, and napping.

The speech therapy exercise today is about counting money, where the therapist gives her an amount, like $42.76, and Kathy has to select the money that makes that amount – she does really well, all things considered. She finishes a crossword puzzle in the evening, with Julia assisting in the writing of the words into the squares. She still has a lot of difficulty with fine motor skills such as writing. According to Julia, she continues to talk in her sleep (but she had no babies last night!). I was at the apartment last night, paying bills, working out, and preparing her medications for post-discharge; and catching an extra hour of sleep.

Her post discharge medications are delivered in the afternoon, since the pharmacy is not open on Saturday, the anticipated discharge day. And, there is a major mix-up on her medications. The medication sheet provided by the transplant team does not match what was delivered. The pharmacy delivered dosing for:

- Both a 75mg of cyclosporine twice per day *and* a 125mg dose twice per day. After some discussion, the extra dosing was removed and confirmed at 125mg twice per day, an increase over previous dosing, but consistent with the past day, when it was increased.
- The micophenolate mofetil was listed on her medication sheet as 500mg, twice per day, but the pharmacy delivered 1000mg, twice per day. After

consulting with the doctors, it was confirmed to be 1000mg, twice per day.

- Her medication sheet also indicated she was to take citalopram, an anti-depressant medication that had been on-again, off-again, due to differing opinions between the transplant team and the neurologist. Eventually, the decision was made that she did not need citalopram, but there it was on the medication sheet. All this was finally corrected and the pharmacist was very helpful and getting the corrections in place, and was apologetic.

This is another lesson – always check the medications provided against the doctor's orders.

Finally, both Kathy and I want to comment on the nursing staff at the step-down unit of the transplant center hospital. They were competent, caring, and compassionate, just wonderful. They worked hard, and it was clear that they took great satisfaction in helping patients get better. The PT, OT, and speech technicians at the rehabilitation hospital were also great, though we did not get the sense that the nurses at the rehabilitation hospital had the same level of dedication as the technicians or the transplant nurses, and they were a bit noisy on the "graveyard" shift. All in all though, the nurses were excellent.

Discharge and Rehabilitation

8

October 17 – Kathy is ready to go home, and we're waiting for the blood tests to come back so she can be discharged, at last. She has a can of Glucerna for breakfast, and a single bite of French toast. We then walk about 300 feet. Kathy naps. Afterward, the nurse goes through the discharge papers with us. We then do some arm exercises, three sets of 10 curls, presses, and triceps, all with one pound weights. Kathy has a mild headache, so we stop and rest. She's also a little nauseous, and has some ginger ale. While we're talking, Kathy recalls the time when the doctors came in just after she had left a trail of diarrhea on the floor on her way to the toilet. We had been asking for immodium for several hours prior to this event to help mitigate the diarrhea, but had been ignored. After this very visual first-hand example where the doctors could literally see her need, she received it very quickly afterward. We had a good laugh over this.

We also discuss and then schedule her in-home rehabilitation. After this discussion, we conclude that she needs physical therapy to develop her strength, both upper body and leg strength. I want a physical therapist to teach me what to do and will handle it from there. We also conclude that she does not need occupational therapy. I can handle that, working with her to do everyday simple things that we all do around the home, like bathe, fold clothing, wash and put away dishes, etc.

Finally, we conclude that speech therapy is her greatest need. Kathy continues to have difficulty with speech, doing simple math, reading, etc., all of which are part of speech therapy. We're advised that someone will contact us at our apartment to set up the schedule for these.

We are finally discharged at noon with instructions to increase Kathy's dose of cyclosporine yet again to 175mg, twice per day. This causes me considerable concern, since this was the dose that was so toxic to her only two weeks ago, inducing encephalopathy and aphasia, and amplifying her trembling. We're hopeful that her body has adjusted to the medication over time, and that her brain has recovered enough from the brain swelling and hemorrhages to tolerate the higher dose.

Kathy rides to the airport with me to put Julia on a plane to go home. She spends over an hour sitting in the car. This is remarkable considering her weakness. Kathy is very sad to see Julia go, and so am I. She has been an extraordinary help to Kathy and me. As discussed previously, I don't know what I would have done without Julia, Liz and Charlie, nor do I know what people do that don't have a good support system when they have a transplant. It must put them at greater risk.

On getting back to the apartment, Kathy walks from the car to the apartment, or about 150 feet. That's 450 feet for the day, and good progress. Later she does upper body exercises like curls, presses, etc. She's pretty tuckered out, so we conclude the day's exercises. Surprisingly, she asks for a McDonald's hamburger, and eats a quarter of it along with five fries. At supper she eats a quarter of a baked potato with butter substitute and sour cream. This is another step forward – she's asking for food. She continues to have some pain, and takes a pain pill, which helps. She seems in a tiny bit better spirits, in spite of the sadness of Julia's departure.

As I'm doing the laundry and preparing dinner, she remarks in a very sad, almost depressed tone, "I don't mean very much to you right now." I cringe and respond with sadness, feeling her pain, "You mean the world to me right now. We'll get through this together." I give her a long, gentle hug. Later, she says that what she meant to say was "I'm not very much help to you right now." I encourage her to focus on helping herself get better and let me worry about the rest. She sleeps fairly well that night, only being up twice with some discomfort, which is helped by a pain pill.

October 18 – We're up at 7am. Her BP is 120/78 and her pulse is 79; temperature is 97.8; glucose is 116, all pretty good numbers. She has her Glucerna and a small bowl of cereal with milk – another step forward toward eating a normal meal. After this she has her medications. So far she seems to be tolerating the increased dose of cyclosporine pretty well. I ask her to hold her hands out, something I'll do several times a day for the next several days to see if the trembling is worse. It's about the same. She's a bit nauseous, and continues to be tired, a normal situation for her. She naps, and then takes a shower with my help. She does most of the work though, which represents more progress. After a rest, she walks 200 feet, rests, and then walks 200 feet again. Then she rests, while drinking another Glucerna. She does not want anything to eat, and I respect this. After the Glucerna, she naps. The rest of the day is pretty calm.

October 19 – We're up at 7am, and her vitals are good. Liz and Charlie arrive at noon or so, and Kathy is perked up by their presence. I think it would be a good thing for her to have frequent company. She's also taking care of most of her bathing now, and is able to walk essentially unassisted. We're always nearby, just in case she "goes wobbly".

We have a very pleasant afternoon with Charlie and Liz, and since they're so are familiar with all the medical terms and practices, we spend considerable time reviewing Kathy's condition and treatment. They seem very pleased with her progress. They were especially complementary to the nursing staff at the Transplant Center.

October 20 – Her vitals are good. Kathy is literally up all day, that is, she takes no naps. She also walks 400 feet in the morning and does more upper body exercises than she's done to date, e.g., four sets of 10 reps for curls, deltoids, triceps, etc.

However, we get some bad news in the afternoon. We're notified that she needs to add a medication, valganciclovir, to treat cyclomegalovirus (CMV). This virus is reported to affect as much as 80% of the population, and the nurse says Kathy had it before the transplant. Unfortunately, for transplant patients whose immune systems are so weak, it is more likely to cause severe infections. Kathy has no fever or other symptoms, but apparently her blood work indicates a very high level of CMV and a problem may be developing. She's put on 900mg of valganciclovir, twice per day.

The medication is $4,814 for a 30 day supply. This is a huge amount to pay, particularly since our insurance policy does not cover medications. The good news is that her micophenolate mofetil is reduced from 1000mg per day to 500mg per day. At least I hope this is good news.

After the in-home physical therapist visit, she is really tired and begins to cry, saying "I don't think I'm going to make it." When she said this a few weeks ago, I was much more concerned than now. I think she's just tired, and maybe a little discouraged with her perception of the lack of progress. It could also be another example of the mood swings from the prednisone. Liz and I reassure her that she's doing fine.

We review with her the progress she's made over the past several weeks. She's now walking several hundred feet per day, and building her arm and leg strength with PT. She's eating more solid food, even asking for certain things. She's talking and thinking more clearly, and even working crossword puzzles with a little help. We encourage her to focus on the progress that she's made to date, and be a little patient. She seems reassured by this.

October 21-23 – We begin in earnest with the physical and occupational therapy. I'm doing most of the physical therapy, but we have a specialist come in twice per week to teach me more techniques and to advise me on the level at which Kathy can function. I tend to push too hard some times, and this training provides a sense of balance for me to know when to ease up.

I also do all of the occupational therapy, those activities that occupy your time on a daily basis, such as brushing teeth, bathing, eating, getting dressed, doing dishes, making a bed, doing laundry, folding clothes and putting them away, etc. These are all the things that we take for granted, but Kathy must relearn them after the transplant. It takes a lot of patience and encouragement. And, we begin intensively on speech therapy, mouth/face exercises, crossword puzzles, and reading, if even only a word or sentence at a time.

One of our favorite pastimes is reading, particularly at bedtime, but Kathy still has a lot of difficulty reading. One night she asks me to read to her. And so we begin what will become a nightly ritual with me reading her to sleep. We begin with Bridge of Sighs, and after that's finished, we continue with Edgar Sawtelle.

I never know when she falls asleep, so the next night we begin with a review of what she remembered last. This is fortuitous, since it also helps with her memory and cognition. It's a touching and memorable activity for us.

A complicating issue for us is that Kathy is very nauseous every morning after a light breakfast, usually oatmeal or cold cereal. This nausea has occurred daily since her discharge a week ago. This requires that every morning after eating she take odansetron, an anti-nausea medication, to minimize the risk of vomiting. She takes most of her medications with food, and if she vomits after eating, she not only loses her meal, but more importantly her anti-rejection medications. So, simply keeping her breakfast down has become a critical issue. A downside of the anti-nausea medication is that it makes her drowsy. When combined with her existing weakness from the disease and trauma she's suffered, she has to nap, every morning, sometimes taking a long one. This is contrary to the Transplant Center's instructions, which we understand are designed to minimize recovery times. However, Kathy not taking a nap is just not realistic yet.

Liz and I conclude, contrary to the instructions in the Gray Book which says no naps during the day, that if she gets a little more rest like short naps, or rest in morning and afternoon, she will be better able to handle the physical and emotional challenges she faces. Our conclusion is that the basic message in the Gray Book is that they don't want you sitting on your butt all day. Kathy certainly does not.

Maybe for a younger patient, this particular rule would work, but we're taking the rules in the context of Kathy's condition and ability, and adapting to that. The important thing is that she's working really hard to get better.

Most of her PT is done in the afternoon, after a light lunch. She walks only a few hundred feet in the beginning, and even this is a struggle. Slowly, but surely, we begin to increase her distance in the coming days. Some days she walks less; some days she walks none at all because she is feeling so bad. If you charted on a graph her distance walked daily, it would look very much like a zigzag or saw tooth, with some days being zero. But, statistically the trend is upward.

October 24 – At one point today, Kathy says "You could be doing something more important, like working with Chevron." (Chevron had contacted me earlier about working with them on a project.) I reply, "I'd rather be here wiping your butt, than meeting with the CEO of Chevron." She smiles and then we both get a laugh out of my comment.

Later that day I get frustrated because she doesn't want to do her upper body exercises, and we have a brief spat. We make up later that day, but I counsel her that she must start taking ownership for her recovery. I can only advise and support. I can't do the hard work of the recovery. I tell her however, that she is the only one who knows how she feels, and the final decision on how much she does is hers and hers alone, and that I'll respect that.

Note to all caregivers, you may get frustrated at times with oppositional behavior while you're trying to help your loved one. These periods come while you're not getting much sleep, all the while generally doing cooking and housework, as well as all your personal affairs like paying bills and handling calls from friends and relatives. It's a hard job. Be patient and loving, in spite of the difficulty.

October 25 – Kathy does not seem to want to do anything today, but she is eating more. Glucerna, however, continues to be the mainstay of her diet.

In the morning she walks 125′, but only in the apartment; and she does 10 side leg lifts, or about 10% of her exercises. She says she's nauseous, and hurting, and so doesn't want to do anything. This is very frustrating for me, seeing her unwilling to do much, except be mesmerized by the TV. Is she really still that sick? Is she regressing? I'm growing to intensely dislike the TV for this. Can you despise an inanimate object? What scares me most is the possibility of seeing her deteriorate, or not grow stronger, in spite of much admonition regarding the risk associated with this. At times, it's like dealing with her mother who is in an assisted living facility, and can be quite oppositional. Now she's watching old time movies, much like her mother does. I hate the thought of living with her like this. There are times when I'm very scared. At one point, she tells me that while watching TV, "At least I know I'm alive." Somehow I'm relieved by this.

In the afternoon, she cries, saying she feels weak, tired, hurting, etc. I say I don't really know what to do, but add "The less you do, the weaker you get; the more you do, the stronger you get." She takes a pain pill, and then later she walks more, and does some upper body exercises – 20 presses, 10 curls, 10 deltoids, and 10 standing-from-sitting.

She then showers, essentially alone, a good thing, and then curls her hair with curlers *for the first time in months*. This takes a lot of effort for her, since she has to lift her arms over her head several times and hold them while curling. We walk to the car and go for a ride. She is feeling a little better. I'm less frustrated and feeling better. My feelings generally mirror her feelings, though we handle our respective emotional states differently. I tend to want to attack the situation or solve the problem. She wants to rest and hope it will resolve itself. Hopefully there's a balance in our approaches that's the right one for her.

October 26 – We drive to the clinic for blood work at 7am and return for breakfast – she has most of a can of Glucerna, plus a half cup of milk and a half cup of cereal, along with her meds. We return later to the clinic for meeting with nurse coordinator and Dr. Z. We wait. Her appointment is for 9am, and we finally see the nurse at 10:15, and Dr. Z at 11am. We work on a cross-word puzzle in the meantime. One clue is "Showed the ropes", and I say "Hung." Kathy laughs. Me too. Well, it is "showing the ropes." Note to all – plan on waiting a lot, as you do for most doctors.

Dr. Z is generally happy with Kathy's condition. Her liver function is still not quite where it should be, but not way out of line. The nurse says drink more water to protect her kidneys. Apparently the medications need to be "flushed" out of your system to reduce the risk of kidney damage. It continues to be difficult to do everything that needs to b e done to get the balance right.

Dr. Z says she must stay on the current meds for a considerable time longer until things stabilize, but does eliminate the iron pills, which make Kathy even more nauseous. He also suggests that she take extra strength acetaminophen as needed.

While we're waiting, Dr. R walks by, waves, and comes back a moment later, saying "I didn't recognize you." As in, you look so much better that I didn't recognize you. It's encouraging to me that he thinks she now looks so much better, but Kathy takes a dimmer view – "I must have looked awful in the hospital," she laments. I tell her she's making good progress.

In the afternoon the speech therapist arrives to begin therapy. I advise her that I don't think we need her any more. Over the past week, I've been working with Kathy doing the things we learned at the therapy center of the rehab hospital. These are mostly simple things like reading out loud, reading silently, doing simple math, pretending to make change from a purchase, mouth muscle exercises, cross word puzzles, sound exercises (much like a voice coach would use for warm up, making various sounds to hit a variety of notes, using vowels a, e, i, o, u), and so on. She tests Kathy and agrees that she doesn't need any more speech therapy. This is really good news. It's only been nine days since her discharge when I thought she needed a lot of speech therapy. We had worried so much about the brain trauma from the brain stem swelling, the seizure and hemorrhages. We are really relieved and pleased with her progress.

October 27 – Kathy's strength is improving. She eats a whole can of chicken noodle soup for supper – a new first. We celebrate the little things around here. I tend to obsess about her food and exercise and we measure everything related to this to determine if she's making progress. My obsession with this sometimes gets in the way of her improving. I'm a "pain in the butt" about it and that sometimes frustrates her. We're still working on getting the balance right for her care.

October 28 – Kathy cried last night because she's missing our two handicapped kids, Jake and Laura, who live in a group home. She wants to go home on Monday, after the blood work, to check on them. She resents the continued inability to do what she could do before she became so ill. I'm so grateful that we have what we have.

My glass isn't half empty, it's half full, **and filling**. I don't enjoy a lot of what I have to do, but I'm grateful to be able to do it and to look forward to the future. I'm not sad about her weakness, I'm grateful she's alive; not disappointed in her pain, but grateful her brain is recovering and that I'm no longer concerned about her going into a nursing home; not depressed about her nausea, but grateful she's eating and talking to me.

Later she puts her hair up in rollers again and after her hair is fixed we go to a local restaurant and get chicken and dumplings to go. She only eats a small portion of the meal, and NO chicken – one of two bites of dumplings, beans, broccoli, apples, and a biscuit.

The good news is that she is actually asking for and eating real food. And, she now works and usually completes the daily crossword puzzle in the paper completely *by herself* – another milestone. We're making progress!

October 29 – We're up at 6:30, but have no TV or internet access – apparently the cable system is down. We have breakfast, and Kathy works on the unfinished crossword puzzle from Monday. It's nearly finished, yet another sign of her continuing recovery. She still has difficulty reading, say a paragraph from a book, but that will come as her brain continues to heal from the brain stem swelling and hemorrhages. She walks to the mailbox and does lots of the physical therapy for strengthening her leg muscles – 15 reps of most all the activities and 10 stand-ups from sitting on the couch. This is really good.

October 30 – Kathy continues to make progress. She's now working the daily crossword puzzle routinely, perhaps not with ease, as she has historically, but it's not the huge burden it had been. Morning nausea continues to be a problem, along with tiredness and pain, but we know she's not pregnant. The pain is chronic, and when combined with tiredness causes her to have less energy than she otherwise would. She's not up for much PT today, only completing about half of her upper body exercises. I accept this and tell her we'll pick it up tomorrow. We're working better together.

October 31 – Kathy is really tired today, napping until about noon. She says "I'm dying", yet again. I gently chastise her to stop acting like her mother and being so histrionic, and suggest that she get up and do something to take her mind off her ills. After a fairly intense discussion, she relents. She walks around the apartment for a few minutes, and then we walk the full hallway and back; and then we walk to the mail box, all in all about 1,000 feet. This is good. In the afternoon, she also does three sets of 10 reps of all her upper body exercises. She is in a much better mood.

November 1 – She is very nauseous in the morning, though she does eat quite a bit – Glucerna, a half cup of cereal and milk each, and a thick slice of bacon. After a nausea pill she naps. No exercise today. The nausea wins.

November 2 – We see the nurse after her blood work. Things seem to be going well (fingers crossed, knock on wood, etc.). In the afternoon we walk nearly a half mile (2,500 feet), a huge distance all things considered. Later the nurse calls to advise her to reduce the cyclosporine to 100 mg, twice per day, versus 125mg. She's now gone from 75 to 125 to 175 to 150 to 125 to 100mg per day in just about two weeks.

Her liver function is still about the same, which is nearly so, but not quite back to normal. The nurse will talk with Dr. R tomorrow and advise us of any further actions or changes.

It's 8pm and Kathy is snoring away at this moment. I hate to wake her, since she's sleeping so soundly, but she must take her meds soon. So, I wake her up and she takes her meds, and then goes right back to sleep. Note to all - It's a really difficult task to keep up with all the medications – they seem to change weekly, sometimes daily, and keeping on top of it all the time is very difficult. Discipline and compliance are critical for a successful transplant outcome, so it is critical to actively and repeatedly review all instructions.

November 3 – Kathy is up again in the middle of the night for the fourth night in a row with the TV on and her TV ears in. Her TV ears are devices that she wears to hear the TV, but without disturbing others, since the volume is low or mute.

She says she tosses and turns in bed and MUST get up. She also says that after she had brain surgery to remove the acoustic neuroma that her ears ring constantly, and so the noise helps her drift off to sleep. I'm thinking that she can't possibly rest or sleep with the TV going and all its associated noise and light. After being up at night, she seems to want to nap much of the day for lack of sleep at night.

This seems to be a bad habit that really upsets me. But, I feel powerless to do anything about it. She has slept just fine when we vacationed in Maine, where there is no TV. My words fall on deaf ears. I thought this habit was broken while she was in the hospital and soon after discharge. I was wrong.

Another setback - the nurse calls to advise that Kathy needs to have an ultrasound done of her liver. Her liver function is not worse according to the lab work, but it's not getting any better either. There is concern that Kathy may have a bile duct blocked, and so this needs to be checked. If this isn't the problem, then another biopsy may be needed. When we get home, Kathy cries, seeing this as another setback in her recovery. I try to reassure her, but I also see it as a setback. We're both worried, but I remind her that we need to take this one day at a time. Her vitals continue to be good. Her strength is improving, along with her appetite. I think these are good signs.

November 4 – Kathy is up yet again for the fifth night in a row in the middle of the night, with the TV on and her TV ears in. Then in the morning she is tired, and as usual gets nauseous after breakfast. This morning we have the ultrasound done of her liver and she is NPO, or nothing by mouth prior to the ultrasound. After the ultrasound, she took most of her meds, except prednisone.

She was nauseous after drinking a Glucerna with her meds, but before taking her prednisone, something we suspect may be causing her nausea. The nausea is a chronic problem. She's does not get sick at night, when she takes most of the same meds, except prednisone, which is only taken in the morning. But, this morning she got sick *before* taking the prednisone. So, it may just be the meds in general, or perhaps just the overall state of her body.

A Brief Visit Home 9

November 5 – After talking with the nurse at the Transplant Center and getting their approval, we travel home for a long weekend. It's the first time in two months. However, we leave only after Kathy does her PT of walking some 1,200 feet with the help of her cane, and then doing various leg strengthening exercises, like long strides, side-, front-, and back-kicks, calf-lifts, and squats. Kathy makes the trip with little problem, though it's late when we arrive and she is quite tired. She makes it up the 15 steps to our bedroom just fine, but makes it clear that she doesn't want to do it again that evening. I smile at her.

We stop at McDonalds on the way home. She seems to like McDonald's now, something that was never the case before. At her request, I've been to McDonald's more in the past week than in the past 10 years. We typically go for a sausage biscuit if it's near breakfast, or for a cheeseburger and fries if it's near lunch or supper. It's not exactly a healthy diet, and it seems contrary to her bouts with nausea. That said, I'm happy to simply see her wanting to eat and enjoying it, even if it is only half of a sausage biscuit. It's more than she has been eating. The doctors, not the dietician, have said that in the short term we should "Let her eat whatever she wants." We're following doctor's orders.

November 6 – We're home and of course we have company – her mother Helen, Aunt Betty, Nadine Andrews (a dear friend), and Liz and Charlie. I'm very protective of Kathy, and have everyone use hand cleaner before coming in, and advising everyone that they can't hug her.

Helen and I have a short tiff about her kissing Kathy. Of course, Kathy is immune-suppressed and at great risk of infection. Helen is in an assisted living facility and exposed to any number of diseases, so I don't want her being too close to Kathy for fear of the risk of infection. I prevail in the argument with Helen, though she is not happy with the outcome, or me. Kathy sits for two hours at a time on the hard bench seats of our kitchen table, which is pretty remarkable in itself, let alone accounting for her condition. She walks in the afternoon with Liz and Charlie and me for 1,500 feet in our neighborhood. My brother and his wife, Randy and Linda, arrive later and we visit even more. She's up and down the stairs twice, or 30 steps. This is really good, considering that three weeks ago she could barely climb 8 steps. She is very tired by the evening and bedtime. We have pizza for supper. She seems to enjoy a piece of pizza. All this represents more progress.

In the middle of all the company, Jake and Laura come for a visit, along with their caregivers at their group home. It's a beautiful moment. Kathy tears up, hugs them, and enjoys their company along with everyone else.

November 7 – We have more company. Randy and Linda spend the morning and early afternoon; her sister Lanie and niece Jenny also come for a short visit; and Sue, our dear friend, arrives for lunch. Lindelle, Sue's husband, arrives in the afternoon. Kathy enjoys all the company. Her mental faculties are clearly improving. Her speech, conversation, articulation, and generally connecting with friends and family is markedly better. I think returning to her home environment is good for her. She seems more at ease and comfortable, and the stimulation is good therapy for her mental well being.

We walk in the afternoon in the neighborhood for about 1,600 feet. In the evening she does her upper body exercises with small two pound weights (she's been using one pound, so I've sneaked these in to see how well she will do) to develop her biceps, triceps and deltoids. She does well with these weights. She's also up and down the stairs twice, another 30 steps.

At the end of the day she is really tired. I later confess that she used two pound weights for her upper body exercise. She gets a little miffed at me. I think it's funny. We kiss. She sleeps well.

Continuing Rehabilitation

10

November 8 – Today we return to the Transplant Center. We finish up breakfast and do some exercises. Kathy walks about 2,000 feet. We finish packing and we're off. We stop at McDonald's, again, about half way to the Transplant Center, and are pleasantly surprised when we run into some old friends from church, Joe and Lynn, and their son. They tell us that he has liver disease as well, but has not been through the transplant qualification process yet. We talk a long time with them. Kathy also has some medications left over from the time prior to her transplant. These medications are no longer necessary or even appropriate, are expensive, and have not expired. So, we offer them to him. Since he's staying temporarily in the same town as the Transplant Center, I promise to get them to him in the next week or so. We get back to our apartment around 4pm.

November 9 – We go for blood work and as usual now, stop for Kathy to have a sausage-egg biscuit and hot chocolate. Her appetite has changed remarkably since the surgery. She likes fast food far more than she has in the past, things like cheeseburgers, macaroni and cheese, bologna, cheese crackers, etc. I keep reminding myself that the doctors have said to let her eat whatever she wants. We'll get to a heart healthy diet after we get food into her that she can keep down. Later in the day we go for a walk at the park. She says she feels weaker than she has, and only walks about 1,500 feet. This is more than her average, but less than her maximum.

Another setback - Later in the day we get a call that she needs yet another biopsy. This is her second since her transplant. Her liver function numbers are significantly worse. It's a huge worry. We say a little prayer. It could be inflammation, auto-immune hepatitis, or rejection. We just don't know. We're going to take things one day at a time.

November 10 – She consumes more protein today, but she still feels jittery, and is worried that the cyclosporine may be inducing another seizure. I've been keeping an eye on her in this regard by making her hold out her hands to see if they're more shaky, observing her walking and doing any number of routine activities to check. It's not obvious to me that there's a big change, but she is feeling it. Constantly observing her behavior is one of my continuing activities. Of course the pending biopsy is a big worry, maybe making her feel jittery. It is me. In the afternoon, we both fold laundry and talk. It's a dreary, rainy, sleepy day. Later she does well on her PT doing some fairly intensive strengthening exercises on her legs, and later does some walking in the apartment building. She falls asleep shortly after taking her meds around 7pm. There's no need to read her to sleep tonight.

November 11 – Her biopsy is today at 10:30. We say a little prayer on the way for God's guidance of the doctors to help Kathy get well. We go in for blood work and then the biopsy. Dr. R says Kathy is doing really well, and outlines certain scenarios to be taken, depending on the biopsy results. I observe that it doesn't feel like she's doing really well, given the need for a biopsy. I advise him of that Kathy is reporting feeling more jittery, at least internally, and that her tremors have increased slightly. She says these feelings are similar to those she had before the seizure in September.

My impression is that she is nowhere near the state she was before the seizure. Her trembling now is very slight, especially compared to what it was September before her seizure, when she was also in a nearly trance-like state. He says we need to continue to pay close attention to this, and alert him to any changes. I also advise she is taking two pain pills on average per day. He seems to think the pain should have dissipated by now and expresses some slight worry that she could become addicted to these. Further, he advises us to suspend the micophenolate mofetil, one of her anti-rejection medications, to allow the valganciclovir to work more effectively in reducing the CMV. It may be resumed later. He also says there should not be any significant risk to her taking two omeprazole per day for her acid stomach. I also mention that she's nauseous every morning, and taking an odansetron for it, but he doesn't express any concern about this; or about her not sleeping well at night, waking up at 3am each morning. For the rash on her arms, he says it's probably eczema and suggests Eucerin. We get some later that day.

After the biopsy results come back, he will be making decisions about what to do next. Her liver function numbers are high, and that could indicate any number of things, such as a blocked bile duct, not withstanding that the ultrasound gave no indication of this, but it's not necessarily conclusive. Or it could be the CMV infecting her liver, or rejection, or inflammation, or some combination. He will advise us after reviewing the results. It's a lot of possibilities to worry about.

November 12 – Kathy has breakfast of cream of wheat and protein supplemented milk, and works on her crossword puzzle. Then she watches TV. A friend and former workmate, David, is coming for dinner that evening.
So, I do a bit of housekeeping – dust, sweep, dishes, etc. After lunch, I help Kathy take a shower, and she is doing more and more of the work in showering. I'm still washing her hair, something I think she likes. I enjoy it too.

After lunch the transplant center calls with the results of the biopsy. She does NOT have any indication of rejection, nor of the CMV infecting her liver, nor of significant inflammation. It's a huge relief, again. Her CMV count has decreased steadily from 22,000 to 1,200 over the past 3 weeks, since she has been on the medication for it. Her liver is "beautiful", according to the doctor doing the biopsy. This is great news, and a huge relief. But, the bad news is that she needs an ERCP to check out her bile and pancreatic ducts, and to clear any blockages or other problems, or to place a stent in the appropriate duct(s). I recall that the ultrasound indicated there were no blockages in her bile duct, but now other tests indicate that there likely is some blockage. The ERCP is scheduled for the next day at 5:30pm.

November 13 – Kathy is on clear liquids for breakfast, and nothing (NPO) after 11am. We arrive at the hospital at 3:30, check in, and wait. You do a lot of waiting when you're in the hospital, and this was no exception. The procedure is scheduled for 5:30. At 4:00pm, they bring Kathy in for prep for the procedure. As she's being wheeled into the operating room, Dr. D, the surgeon, is coming down the hall and makes a bit of fun at our kissing good bye. Kathy tells him jokingly to "mind your business".

The procedure is over in half an hour and Kathy now has a stent in her bile duct, which Dr. D says was occluded. This occlusion resulted in bile backing up into her liver, causing its function to deteriorate. The stent should alleviate the problem and provide adequate bile flow.

He also says the stent will need to be removed in 3 months, and that another may be put in then. This could go on for a year, but that remains to be seen. He didn't find any other problems. This is good news.

We get home at 1am, after a six hour post-op waiting period to make sure there are no other problems induced by the procedure, like pancreatitis. Kathy is placed on levofloxacin, an antibiotic, for the next five days to reduce the risk of infection. She's also put on ursodiol again to help the bile duct function. It apparently "lubricates" the bile duct and/or reduces the viscosity of the bile to facilitate bile flow and prevent it from backing up into the liver. This was one of her pre-transplant medications when she was thought to have primary biliary cirrhosis, which affects the bile ducts.

November 14 – This is a recovery day from yesterday's procedure, but Kathy must be feeling better. She's getting much better at giving orders, while she sits on the couch and I do all the work. I resent this just a little at times, but I'm also grateful that she feels good enough to be a little bossy.

I'm off to Walmart this morning, while she works her crossword puzzle. Here's hoping the stent does the trick for getting her liver function back to normal. She has not done very much PT or walking this week, and may have lost some of what she had gained. We'll see on Tuesday when the physical therapist is supposed to give her the final round of PT and test her to assure that she can be discharged from further formal PT.

November 15 – Kathy seems to have more energy today. She was up during the night looking for something to eat – bite sized candy bar, crackers and ginger ale. Her weight is down to 124 pounds. She gets her own cereal and milk this morning, something I usually do, and so that's another first.

She naps, and then showers. I continue to help with washing her hair. She rolls her hair with ease now, another sign of progress. She has soup and Glucerna for lunch.

Then we go shopping at Michaels, a craft store, and get things for the grandkids when they visit on Thanksgiving, such as coloring books, reading books, and puzzles. She stands, walks, and shops for more than 20 minutes. Afterwards, we go find the party rental place, where I'll be picking up extra chairs and furniture for the grandkids visit, and then we go on to the park. We walk about 100 yards, and then sit and talk for a while, and return. It's a beautiful fall day, sunny, warm, and very pleasant. We return and she works on her crossword puzzle.

She remembers that she hasn't taken her antibiotic after lunch. This is another sign that she's getting better, since I've been looking after the medications. Or, maybe it's a sign that I'm getting worse. I shouldn't be letting this happen, so it's good that she caught it. Medications are critical. She finishes working her crossword puzzle, yet another good sign.

November 16 – Kathy was up again last night having a snack. She is still obsessed with getting up and sleeping on the couch. One excuse is as good as any other. I forget what last night's was, pain I think, but it could have been hunger. I hate this. And, it concerns me greatly that she is damaging her hearing by having the earphones in her ears **all night long**, every night. This habit simply was not broken when she was in the hospital. I plan to disable the TV at night in the next few days to see if that will work in getting her to stay in bed for the night.

She had her blood work and doctor appointment this morning. Her prednisone was reduced from 15mg to 10mg per day; and she was taken off nystatin, a liquid medication that she's been taking four times per day to minimize the risk of a fungal infection in her mouth. Almost nonchalantly, the doctors tentatively set December 7th as the day when we can move back home. That is, they're no longer concerned that she needs to be nearby for treatment. We're going home. It doesn't seem real just yet. Maybe it will in three weeks.

In the afternoon, her liver function numbers were reported as slightly better, another good sign. We hope that as time passes, her prednisone will go to zero, her micophenolate mofetil will go to zero, and that she will no longer need blood pressure medication.

In the afternoon we have an appointment with her neurologist. When he finally comes into the examination room, I introduce Kathy to him – "Dr. S2, I'd like you to meet the new Mrs. Moore. The last time you saw her, she was in Paris." He smiled. The last time he saw Kathy, in the hospital, he asked her where she was, and she replied, "Paris." He indicates that he will order an MRI in the coming weeks to check her brain and brain stem, indicating it's not urgent. If that comes out well, she may get to come off the anti-seizure medication. Getting her off all these meds would be a blessing. Note to all – on leaving the hospital most transplant patients are on a LOT of medication, but with time, many of these may be suspended as progress is made. As noted, it is *critical to have discipline in keeping track of the medications*, and complying with all the requirements, particularly as they change, which can occur weekly, or even daily.

I send an email to friends and family:

All -

A quick update. Kathy continues to make progress. The transplant team had another liver biopsy done on Wednesday, Nov 11th, after some of her liver "numbers" indicated a significant deterioration in performance. Fortunately, the biopsy results indicated that the liver is "beautiful", to quote the pathologist, and that there was no indication of any infection.

Unfortunately, it also indicated a high bile level in the liver, suggesting bile duct malfunction or blockage. To check and correct this, she had an ERCP (Endoscopic Retrograde Cholangiopancreatography – that's why it's called an ERCP), on Friday evening, and a stent was installed into her bile duct to provide for unobstructed flow. We expect this will resolve the problem and allow her liver to return to normal, though that may take a few days.

At our appointment this morning at the transplant clinic, her prednisone dose (anti-rejection) was decreased from 15mg to 10mg per day; and a drug called nystatin was discontinued – no longer needed. At our appointment with the neurologist this afternoon, he said she had made remarkable progress, but would still like to do an MRI to make sure there are no residual issues with her brain from the previous trauma.

She continues to make good progress from a physical therapy view and we expect that her in-home PT will end this week, though she still has a long way to go to get back to truly normal. She's basically back to normal from a social interaction view – reading, working crossword puzzles and doing normal day-to-day things, though her energy level is still quite low. That will improve with as we increase her activity in the coming months.

At this point we're hopeful that her liver will soon stabilize and we can go home in early December, with continued checkups to be done in Knoxville, as well as routine trips back to the transplant center.

Please continue keep her (and the donor/family) in your thoughts and prayers, since organ rejection can happen at any time, particularly during the first 6 months. Thank you all so very much for your support. It continues to be a real blessing.

Ron and Kathy

PS – Kathy dries and curls her hair with ease now – a sure fire sign she's getting better.

We got a lot of encouraging and funny comments back from our friends regarding Kathy now being able to dry and curl her hair. It made us both smile.

November 17 – Kathy had a snack again last night, another good sign that she's getting her appetite back. This morning she's in reasonably good spirits. She has a good breakfast and then does her crossword puzzle.

After we watch a bit of TV, we go to the fitness center. She walks there, then up the steps, all 15 of them, then spend six minutes on the recumbent bike, and then walks a couple minutes on the treadmill. Then we walk home. Overall it's a good session. She's now tired and napping.

Later we're off to bring some of Kathy's left over pre-transplant medications to our friend's son from church that we ran into at McDonald's, that is, lactulose, spironolactone, rifaximin, and neomycin. We bring others, like tacrolimus and nystatin that Kathy can no longer use and are left over post-transplant, to a person that manages unused medications and tries to get them to those in need, or disposes of them properly.

The PT lady arrives at 4pm to test Kathy for her physical strength. Kathy passes with flying colors. She discharges Kathy from further formal PT. More progress!

November 18 – This is a good day with PT, walking, reasonable meals, and good conversation with Kathy.

November 19 – This is generally a bad day. Kathy had nausea all day long, though without any vomiting. Not much is done in the way of PT, walking or meals. Conversation was limited. Hopefully tomorrow will be a better day.

November 20 – This is a good day. In the evening we have dinner with the Tim and Mary, some friends who live not far from the Transplant Center. This is *our first evening out in over a year*. It is a wonderful evening of just talking, having a meal and enjoying the company of others. Kathy's energy holds up well.

November 21 – It's a good day. We went to *church together for the first time in about nine months*, and then out to a local restaurant for an evening meal. Wow – that's *two days in a row with an evening out!* Of course, we came home early.

November 22 – It's a slow day. Morning nausea continues to be an everyday thing. Not much walking or other activities today.

November 23 – It's generally a good day. She walks more than a half mile.

November 24 – The day does not begin well. She has a breakfast of a sausage biscuit at 7am, takes her meds at 8am, and then throws up at 9am. She's naps after vomiting. We're advised that if you don't see the meds in their solid form in the vomit, then you do not take the meds again. If you do see them in solid form, you take the meds again. She doesn't take them again, but it concerns me as to how much medication got into her system. Rejection is a constant worry.

We later go for a ride to return her wheelchair to the medical devices company. She is confident it's no longer necessary. She had been using the wheelchair on occasion as a backup or in the event she got tired while we were walking. This represents more progress.

Later we go shopping at Walmart. She walks about 2000 feet, which is good, considering she threw up this morning. And, we go food shopping in preparation for Thanksgiving with our son and his family. We're looking forward to seeing them, especially the five grandkids.

November 25 – It's a pretty ordinary day, but better than yesterday, since she's only mildly nauseous, but having no vomiting. Our son Ken, his wife Joanne, along with grandkids Nathalie, Tom, Jack, Paul, and Melodie, are arriving tonight to celebrate Thanksgiving with us. We're very grateful for their visit. Kathy walks over half a mile before they arrive. Unfortunately, they arrive too late that evening to visit.

November 26 – It's Thanksgiving Day! Clearly, we have a lot to be thankful for, and in spite of some early nausea for Kathy, it's a very good day. We have a really good visit with Ken, Joanne and all the kids. As usual, we have a large meal, squeezing everyone into our tiny one bedroom apartment, making do with folding chairs and tables. It's a bit chaotic, and wonderful. After dinner we go to the apartment recreation center that we had rented for the day to allow for a little more play room. Then later, we make a trip to the local park where we play ball, tag, and all the other things kids do at the park. It was great. Kathy doesn't feel well enough to take the trip to the park with us, but still has a good visit with everyone. That evening, we have a party for Tom, one of the grandkids, who coincidentally has his birthday tomorrow. A good time was had by all.

November 27 – Ken and Joanne and the grandkids join us in the morning to visit for a short while and then say goodbye. They're off to visit friends who live a couple hours away. It's so nice to have them around, and the grandkids are wonderful to be with. They warm our hearts. Kathy takes a nap after lunch. Later she feels well enough to walk over a half mile in the park. Then we go shopping. It's a good day, and represents more progress.

November 28 – We have a slow morning, she has a nap after lunch, then we go for a long walk of nearly a mile in the park on a beautiful, cool fall day. This is as far as she has walked at one time since the transplant. Later, we go shopping for jeans. I fix a casserole for dinner. It's a very nice day.

November 29 – We go for a walk in the park, and then drive to a small local college with a lovely campus, and go for another walk. Kathy walks about a mile again today. It's continuing progress and another nice day.

November 30 – We go to the clinic for routine blood work, and then see the nurse, and the PA. We go back to our apartment for a while, and then to see a movie, Blind Side, a true story of a homeless kid who is adopted by a family and goes on to play for the NFL. It's a good movie, very uplifting, and it fits nicely into our day, since it's *our first movie in over a year*. It's a dreary, rainy, wet, cold day, and it's also wonderful.

December 1 – It's a slow day. She has breakfast, then naps, and then works a crossword puzzle. She is increasingly proficient working these puzzles, another indication of progress. Then we're off to a local restaurant for lunch. Unfortunately, she's a bit nauseous after lunch and takes another nap. Later, we go for a walk in the park for about 3,000 feet. All in all, it's a pretty good day.

December 2 – Kathy has a headache all day long, and is nauseous most of the day. There's no walk today. It's a bummer of a day.

December 3 – Nausea is a standard event, every morning. Kathy feels well enough by mid-morning to shower, and afterwards is well enough to go to a local town that's supposed to be having a Christmas street festival. It turns out that we're a day early and so the festival hasn't really begun. We still have a nice walk through the downtown area, and a pleasant lunch. We do get to see the ginger bread houses. A lot of work goes into these. It's a good day.

December 4 – Kathy is nauseous most of the day. I have a meeting with a client who happens to live near the Transplant Center. After lunch Kathy takes a nap. Late in the afternoon, we go for a walk at a local strip mall to the Post Office and a drug store. It's a pleasant enough walk, but Kathy is still not feeling well today.

December 5 – More nausea, in spite of trying some different foods that we think will be easy on her stomach, like rice milk with a protein supplement. It's very frustrating for both of us, but especially for her, since she has to suffer through it. I wish we knew what to do to eliminate or minimize the nausea. Right now the only thing that seems to work is the odansetron, but she hates having to take it every day.

Going Home 11

December 6 – We're going home tomorrow, nearly three months after leaving. We spend the day mostly packing and cleaning the apartment. It's exciting, and a bit scary. We won't be near the Transplant Center any more, and so if a problem develops, their expertise will likely have to come via telephone. While this is not the best of circumstances for a transplant patient, we're going home. It's an acceptable risk.

December 7 – We finish packing and turn in our keys to the apartment manager, saying goodbye to her and her staff. They have been wonderful people during our entire stay, helping in anyway they could. Our car is fully loaded, packed to the ceiling and with a very full trunk, with all the "stuff" we have to move back home. It's amazing what you can accumulate in about 12 weeks, even after giving part of it away and throwing away disposable stuff.

The trip home is uneventful. I had some concern before we left that it would be very tiring for Kathy, but she couldn't simply crawl into the back seat and rest or take a nap, since it was completely full to the ceiling. She makes the trip with no problems, but is very tired when we get home. I go about unpacking the things that require immediate attention. I'll do the rest tomorrow.

December 8-16 – Since moving back home on December 7, we've been busy re-settling. During that time, Kathy's nausea has continued, but seems to be easing off some. She has been skipping her anti-nausea medicine on some days, and is eating more regular food. Fast food continues to be a favorite though.

The good news is that she is not having much trouble getting her 60 or so grams of protein per day, but she rarely exceeds the 60 grams by very much. The bad news of course is that fast food carries a lot of fat with it. More good news is that she's been much more active in the home, helping cook simple meals, doing laundry, and working on the company books. While we're not doing nearly as much walking as we had been, this is mitigated by the shopping trips and walking in the stores and supermarkets. So, it's not a worry. We're simply trying to return to a normal life.

On December 10, I send out the following email to friends and family:

> Hi Everybody –
>
> *We're home!* Kathy was released to return home, and we arrived this past Monday. Since then we've been working to re-settle in our home. I was surprised at how much "stuff" you can accumulate in just three months in a one bedroom furnished apartment, that you then have to deal with when you get home.
>
> More importantly, Kathy's liver and kidney function as of Monday were ALL in the normal range for the first time in a decade. While she still has daily morning nausea (I'm confident it's NOT morning sickness), we're encouraged by everything else, and very glad to be home. We'll continue to have weekly blood work here to monitor her condition, with monthly trips for the next few months to the Transplant Center for checkups there; and we'll continue to help build her strength in the coming months.
>
> By the way, we highly recommend the Transplant Center to anyone needing a transplant. Not withstanding a few issues of concern, we felt that overall the Transplant Center there did an outstanding job – excellent physicians and PA's, surgeons, hospital nursing care and rehabilitation.

Given our circumstances, we haven't gotten to the usual written Christmas cards this year, something I much prefer. So, please accept this note with our very best wishes to you all for a very Merry Christmas and a happy, healthy, prosperous new year. All the best to everyone.

Ron (Dad/Grampa) and Kathy (Nanna)

December 17-24 – We continue to try to re-establish our life into the normal that we once knew. It's not likely to ever be quite the same as it was, say five years ago, but we believe we can come close. We continue to measure and log her daily blood pressure, glucose, and heart rate; and I'm notionally tracking her protein and calorie consumption, just to make sure she gets the minimum a 40+ grams of protein per day and about 1,500 calories. Life is also pretty busy trying to catch up with Christmas shopping, visiting, and generally being "normal" at Christmas, whatever that is. Personally I'm glad Christmas only comes once per year. It's pretty hectic, particularly with helping Kathy, AND trying to do the normal Christmas stuff. We limited our shopping this year to mostly gift cards. Kathy wasn't up to it, and frankly I don't enjoy it. More importantly, we didn't want to expose Kathy to all the crowds and their associated germs and disease, since she is immuno-suppressed.

During this time, we have lots of company, including Kathy's sisters and their husbands and children, most who live locally. Our daughter Lisa and her husband Blake, along with grandkids Tarisa and Dakota, come for a visit all the way from Texas. It's been a long time since we've gotten together, and we enjoy it very much. Later, daughter Pam and husband John, along with grandkids Andrew and Devin come; and daughter Trish and husband Carlos, along with grandkids Harley, Maria, and Sydney; come for a visit.

Pam and Trish are much closer, in Alabama, so we see them more often, but it's always a pleasure to have family around, especially the grandkids. I'm not sure why, but there's a different kind of love that comes with a grandchild, kinder and gentler.

During this time I write a letter to the family of the donor. This is a *very* difficult letter to write, one thanking them for the gift of life in their sacrifice, but knowing their loved one had to die to provide that gift. That gift is Christ-like, that is giving your life so that others may live. In a very real sense a part of their loved one is still alive. I hope they can take some comfort in that. I will deliver the letter to the Transplant Center on our next visit. The protocol is that donor families and recipients do not know each other, and communication is handled through the Transplant Center.

December 25-27 – It's a quiet Christmas. The kids are all at their homes celebrating Christmas with the grandkids, as it should be. We're simply grateful to be home and have Kathy alive and doing well. Our gift to each other this year is simply being together.

December 28 – We visit the Transplant Center for Kathy's three-month checkup and see the nurse coordinator, the PA, and the surgeon, Dr. E. With this visit, Dr. E will be turning over Kathy's care to her Hepatologist, Dr. R. I give Dr. E two letters. One is a "thank you" letter which thanks everyone for the great job they did, and is to be shared with everyone. The second is for her doctors only. It details some of our less-than-positive experiences, and offers suggestions for ways they might avoid these or make them better for future patients. All the sessions go very well, and they are pleased with her progress. With the PA's approval, we discontinue metoprolol, one of her blood pressure medications.

Kathy has another MRI, which indicates that she is getting much better. The brain stem swelling is nearly gone, and the hemorrhages are also nearly resolved. She's improved enough that we can suspend the anti-seizure medication. There are still a few minor abnormalities, but these are not considered serious and should completely resolve in time. More progress!

December 29-January 2 – Things are fairly normal for the next few days. After discontinuing the metoprolol, Kathy's BP increased from about 100/60 to about 115/75, which was still fine. However, we also noticed that her pulse jumped up to 105-110, or more, where it had been 75-80, a jump of 30 beats per minute. She has also been feeling more jittery and tired. So, we re-started the metoprolol and her BP immediately dropped back to about 100/60 and perhaps as importantly, her heart rate dropped back to 75-80, or normal. She's also much less jittery and tired. I suspect a sustained heart rate of 115bpm will make you more tired and jittery, since it's a bit like jogging a slow jog all day long (that's my heart rate when I'm walking fast or early in a slow jog). Later, I do a little research on metoprolol and find that it should be gradually decreased, not suddenly stopped, as we did. This was not mentioned by the staff at the Transplant Center when they said she could discontinue it. It's another lesson learned.

January 3-24 –. *Further complications are also developing.* We continue to monitor her blood pressure, heart rate, glucose levels, and have her weekly blood checks. The medications continue to have a negative impact on her immune system. Two indicators, of several, are her white blood count, and her absolute neutrophils, which continue to decline. After the January 11 blood work, the Transplant Center orders discontinuing mycophenolate mofetil, one of her anti-rejection medications, apparently because it has had a very negative impact on her white blood cell count.

Her red blood also count continues to decline. From her blood tests of January 18, her hemoglobin is down to 8.2 (normal is 12-16) and her hematocrit is down to 23 (normal is 37-47). Perhaps more scary is that her blood's cyclosporine level, her primary anti-rejection medication, is down to 58, well below the therapeutic level. At this point after the transplant, the Transplant Center wants this to be between 150 and 200 in order to minimize the risk of rejection. This is a sudden and dramatic drop from a level of about 150, where it had been running. Her cyclosporine dose is increased to help get her blood levels back into the therapeutic range.

A small bit of good news is that Dr. S2, her neurologist, advises us that after reviewing the MRI scan in more detail, Kathy can gradually wean herself from the anti-seizure medication, levetiracetum, and so we begin that process.

January 25 – We go in for blood work, and are particularly concerned about bringing Kathy's cyclosporine levels to a therapeutic level to prevent rejection, and about her red blood and white blood counts. So far we've don't have any indications of rejection, even with the low levels indicated in her blood tests. At this point Kathy is VERY tired and often breathless. Her red blood count is so low that it apparently is not sufficient to supply adequate oxygen to her body. Yet, she continues to try to walk some every day, even 15 minutes at a very slow pace. Unfortunately, the medications that prevent rejection and other problems, like CMV infection, also have a very negative effect on white and red blood counts and so these must be monitored regularly. It's delicate balance that must be managed with great attention to detail. I'm worried.

A Crisis   12

January 26 – We visit Dr. S for the first time since last August. He's her local physician in Knoxville. He thinks she's making good progress, but notes that her red blood count is getting dangerously low. He orders a transfusion of two units of blood, a seemingly straightforward order.

January 27 – This will turn out be a very bad day. On our way to get the blood transfusions, we get a call from the Transplant Center, advising Kathy to stop taking valganciclovir, the medication for treating her CMV. As noted previously, it's a common virus in the US population, which can infect and kill transplant patients because of their suppressed immune system. Kathy's CMV is now zero, or more accurately, non-detectable. The medication also has the side effect of destroying your red blood count, as well as your white blood count, making you much more subject to *other* diseases. At this point Kathy's hemoglobin is 6.7, well below normal, and her hematocrit is 18.6, also well below normal. Not only this, but her white blood count is down to 1.3 (normal is 4.8 – 10.8), and her absolute neutrophil is critically low at 0.2 (normal is 1.7 – 6.5), *making her much more susceptible to infection.*

No one told us of these limits, so we were not aware of the need to pay closer attention as she approached this level and take preemptive action. We were advised with a vague suggestion to see a hematologist as Kathy's blood count deteriorated, but no criteria were given. It would have been nice to know then what we know now. Another lesson is learned.

All this seems like you're damned if you do, and damned if you don't. It's really hard to get the balance right, and it varies from patient to patient. Perhaps as importantly, the doctors and other hospital staff can't possibly remember everything that might affect a patient, and sometimes they do not think at a systems level, understanding all the interactions of various treatments, medications, and varying patient's responses to all these. *It is essential that both patient and caregiver be intimately involved in the treatment process, understand the side effects of the medications, and constantly question the treatments and medication to assure the best possible outcome.*

Kathy is getting her two units of blood now. An interesting question arose prior to her transfusion. Should she receive blood that has been treated to eliminate the CMV in it? My initial response was yes, since we had spent months, and some $18,000 on a specific medication to get her CMV to a zero reading.

It seemed to me that giving her blood infected with CMV would not be wise. My thinking was apparently incorrect, since the Transplant Center said she had developed antibodies to it, and it would be OK to receive either type, that is, with or without CMV. In any event the blood she was given had been treated to eliminate the CMV.

After the transfusion of two pints, Kathy seems to be doing fine. She has a low grade fever of about 100, which is common in a transfusion, and she had a low grade fever just before the transfusion of 99.4. We thought it was just because of the nervousness and walking to the clinic, but that may not have been true. As the evening progressed she gradually develops chills and a fever of 102.1; her BP is 145/86 and her pulse is 125.

After talking with the nurse on call at the Transplant Center, I give her some acetaminophen and benadryl at 10pm, and by 1am her fever is down to 100.2; her BP is about 110/67, and her pulse is 94. I think she is on the mend, and am very relieved.

January 28 - My optimism is not well founded. By 4am, she is vomiting, has chills, and her fever is 103.1; her BP is 124/82, and her pulse is also back up to 124. I call the Transplant Center again, and at their direction, we go to the local hospital ER. Her fever declines a bit during that time to 101.4.

Dr. F in the ER speaks to Dr. H4 at the transplant center, and as a precaution, they preemptively treat her for an infection using an array of antibiotic and antiviral medications, given at different times and in a particular sequence according to protocol. These include ceftazidime, levofloxacin, vancocin, and piperacillin-tazolbactam, just in case she does have an infection, which should show up in the cultures being done.

Unfortunately, her immune system is in such poor condition, it would be highly risky to wait to treat her if she does have an infection. They are also considering giving her filgrastim to stimulate her white count and neutrophils and thus increase her immune response. By night her temperature is low-grade at about 100.

Preliminary tests do not provide any evidence of any known bacterial infection, but we won't have the cultures back for another 12-36 hours. Her immune system is pretty depressed – her white blood count this morning was 0.4, and her absolute neutrophil was 0.2, both critically low. But, following the transfusions, her hematocrit is better at 29; hemoglobin is also better at 10.

We're both very worried. She's had several transfusions previously at the Transplant Center with no problems that we're aware of, though she was not nearly as immune-suppressed.

Now we have a great deal of concern. Is this a reaction to one of the units of blood? Or, could it truly be an infection caused by a very low level of bacteria in the blood that quickly took advantage of her very poor immune system? Or, is it some sort of alteration of her immune system due to the transfusion? Or, is it something else, or even some combination of these issues? We would like to understand this event better as to its possible causes, so we can work to minimize the risk for this in the future.

We send our questions to the Transplant Center. Unfortunately, I really don't know enough to be able to ask the right kind of questions, but I give it a try:

1. Should more detailed specifications be provided for her blood requirements based on her specific condition, e.g., white count, neurophils, etc., so that, for example, irradiated blood is used, e.g., non-CMV or with-CMV, or some other appropriate specification?
2. Would it be possible to trend certain parameters such that better statistical limits or data were established so that *dis*continuing certain medications could be accomplished in a more timely manner, one that is appropriate before her immune system becomes as depressed as hers? There are software programs available to support this kind of statistical analysis.
3. Kathy and I are both O+. Given that our blood is compatible, would it be appropriate, if she needs another transfusion, for me to donate blood in advance in sufficient time so that she could receive

it? Presumably we have very similar antibodies and disease resistance given our long history of living together.

4. Has she had an alloreaction to the blood? She has had 4 units prior to the transplant, about 35 units during the transplant, and 4 units post transplant while in the hospital. My understanding is that an alloreaction occurs when the body builds up an antibody response to even minor mismatches in some of the blood proteins that may not be caught in its screening, and a reaction occurs. How can this risk be better managed?

The Transplant Center responds that it's ok to check my blood and use it if it's compatible with hers. They also say they don't have anything to add to my questions and that they use a best practice standard.

This is **not** a very satisfying answer from a group that I respect and admire. I'm hoping for answers, not "boiler plate". I deal with so-called best practices in manufacturing, and my view is that "best practice" is not necessarily a rigid set of rules requiring strict adherence. The principles embodied within the rules may require strict adherence, but best practice is constantly evolving to adapt to improved technology, skills, practices and the learning that is developed along the way. Kathy's experience, and in fact all patients' experiences, should be viewed as a learning opportunity.

We find out later from Steve, a friend of ours who has a PhD in microbiology and specializes in human immune responses, that Kathy should likely have been pre-treated with acetaminophen, benadryl, and a shot of steroids, given her history of blood transfusions, a total of more than 40 units prior to this transfusion.

Later, Kathy's hematologist also indicates that individuals who have had multiple units of blood in the previous several months should likely be pre-treated in this manner. If only we had known. Another lesson is learned.

I contact the transfusion center and ask them why they did not pre-treat Kathy before the transfusion. They say that the doctor should order this. My reply is that they should be asking the question as an additional measure of quality control, and to avoid future risk to other patients, and to them. I don't know if this ever happened. Incidentally, it's Kathy's birthday. This is not a good way to celebrate.

January 29 – Kathy's temperature is back to normal. Her blood pressure is now about 100/60, and her pulse is around 80, all good numbers for her. The day is fairly boring – more IV's of anti-biotics and anti-virals, and waiting. Dr. A, an infectious disease doctor, stops by on rounds. He seems quite satisfied with the regimen she's on. Dr. F, her hematologist, also comes by. He wants to give her another unit of blood – her hematocrit is down to 24, from 29 yesterday, and her hemoglobin is also down to 8.5. Both of these decreases could be due to the increase in the volume of her blood from all the IV's.

So, for now Kathy declines another transfusion, suggesting we wait to see how things evolve. Dr. F does prescribe filgrastim for stimulating an increase in her white blood count and immune system, and epoetin alpha for stimulating her red blood count. The filgrastim will require a few days to take effect, but the epoetin alpha will take weeks to be fully effective. There is still no indication of specific infection from the cultures taken on Thursday morning, the 28th.

While in the hospital we insist on maintaining control of and giving Kathy all her medications related to the transplant, that is, her anti-rejection medications, ursodiol, and so on. The hospital staff is initially not comfortable with this, but we meet with the doctor in charge of Kathy's care and explain our reasoning:

1. The hospital does not handle transplant patients and is not familiar with the medications required.

2. We do not want to risk that they may change brands of anti-rejection medication. Different brands have different efficacies and we have been advised by the Transplant Center *not* to change brands.

3. Hospitals tend to give medications in certain two hour bands of time, or longer if they are really busy with emergencies. We wanted to make sure Kathy adhered strictly to taking her medications every 12 hours.

The doctor concurred, noting that they would continue to manage her additional medications related to the infection and hospitalization. Of course, we agreed with this. The nursing staff was kind enough during their rounds to remind Kathy to take her meds. She always had, but it was a nice double check.

January 30 – We're still waiting. Kathy's temperature is now slightly below normal at 98 or so, and stable; her BP is 85/58, or low; and her pulse is 79. These are all good signs. There is still some concern regarding a possible infection of claustridium dificil, or C-dif, in her intestine, so she'll be providing a stool sample for a test for that. They have also started a pro-biotic to restore some of the good bacteria in her intestine.

Her blood work from today indicates improvement in the white blood count. It's now 1.0, and her absolute neutrophils are 0.66. This is much better than the 0.4 and 0.2 numbers from Monday – Wednesday, but is still well below the minimum requirement of 1.5 for WBC and 1.0 for absolute neutrophils, which is still well below the minimum normal range of 4.0 and 2.5, respectively. Her hemoglobin has also dropped from 8.5 to 7.5 and her hematocrit is down from 24 to 21. This is likely due to some dilution from the 24-hour saline IV's. The doctors didn't tell us this, but Liz did, suggesting that we not become too alarmed about this yet.

Nonetheless, Kathy is likely to get another transfusion tomorrow. Our hope at this point is that now that she is off micophenolate mofetil and valganciclovir, their effects will diminish over the coming weeks, and that the filgrastim and epoetin alpha will help her system stimulate the white and red blood counts.

We still have considerable concern about the level of cyclosporine in her blood, which continues to hover around 60 for no apparent reason, and in spite of increased dosing from 125 mg twice per day to 200 mg twice per day. She's hasn't shown any signs of rejection, at least not yet. We have our fingers crossed, are knocking on wood, and saying our prayers, an odd combination in itself.

January 31 – Kathy's blood count has improved considerably. Her WBC is now 1.8, vs. 1.0 yesterday, and 0.4 the day before. This is still less than half of the low end of the normal range, but substantially better than it was. But, her red blood count is only slightly improved. Her hemoglobin is at 7.7 versus 7.5 yesterday, and her hematocrit is still 21, about half of the low end of normal.

So, the decision is made to give her another transfusion. This time she is pre-treated prior to the transfusion, which is CMV negative, not withstanding the transplant center saying its ok for her to have CMV positive. And, she's being given O-blood, though she's O+. When I questioned this, the answer was that O- is the universal donor, and there was no O+ in the blood bank that was CMV negative. Somewhere from deep in the cobwebbed passages of my brain I remember that O- is the universal donor.

She seems to be taking the transfusion well. So far her temperature isn't even slightly elevated, something that happened on Wednesday, and is also common. This simply re-emphasizes the point about continuously asking questions. They give her another unit of blood at 10pm, which is O+ this time. She has no reaction to this one either. Her temperature is 97.6 or so during the entire transfusion, and during the night.

With her white blood count being so low, Kathy is neutropenic and at high risk of infection. As such this requires people to wear a mask and wash and/or clean their hands before coming into her room. However, I've noticed that some people do and some do not adhere to these rules. The cleaning staff do. They even wear gowns before entering. One nurse that was treating Kathy cleared her throat several times. I asked if she should be treating Kathy without having a mask. She ignored me, finished her task and left. My general observation is that if you have rules, they should be clear, and people should follow them. I meet with the floor nurse to express my concerns and later will write a letter to her, copying it to the president of the hospital, admonishing them for not following their own protocols. That's discussed later.

February 1 – Kathy's white cell count is up to 3.1, meaning her absolute neutrophils are now about 2.0, nearly 10 times better than they were on Monday. The infectious disease doctor seems pleased with the result, and plans to wean Kathy from the antibiotics she is currently on, going to pill form by tomorrow morning. Given that she continues to improve, he says we should get to go home tomorrow. When asked, he wouldn't comment on her red blood count. This is just one more indication that doctors tend to focus on their specialty. He suggests that we talk with the hematologist about this.

February 2-6 – Kathy is discharged from the hospital on February 2nd, a long and arduous process. She continues to recover in the coming days from her illness, but we still don't know the cause, whether it was from a transfusion reaction or an infection. The cultures were all negative for an infection, even though an infection was indicated by her high fever. It could also have been an alloreaction to the blood transfusions. It could have been a simple stomach infection. She ate a pimento cheese sandwich for lunch which included mayonnaise, and mayonnaise is notorious for causing infections. We'll never know, but an absence of evidence is not evidence of absence.

February 7 – We travel to the Transplant Center for blood work, meeting with the nurse coordinator and PA; and for an ERCP to replace the stent in Kathy's common bile duct.

February 8 – She has her blood work and we meet with the nurse and PA. Nothing particularly abnormal shows up at this point, and in fact her cyclosporine level is at 160 this week and was 180 last week, right in the middle of the current desired range of 150-200. This is dramatically better than ~60 that it had been at for the previous three weeks.

We still don't know why her cyclosporine would suddenly drop. There is no apparent reason. She did not drink grapefruit juice or eat grapefruit, or change the brand of medication being used, or do anything that we're aware of that would have caused this. In fact her routine and medications were strictly in compliance with all the doctor's orders. The PA did note that her AST and ALT, her liver enzymes, were elevated, but he did not express any concern.

The ERCP goes well, and the doctor advises us to see him again in three months, though he mentions an abnormality in the common duct, but said that could wait three months, after more scar tissue has formed, and that he would then know what to do, if anything. Interestingly, the procedure was at 4pm, she was out of the operating room by 5pm, and released to go home at 6pm. When the stent was first put in, she had to stay until midnight or so. The doctor said he did not do as invasive a procedure this time, since looking at the pancreatic ducts was not necessary, and so the risk of pancreatitis was not as great. So, we can leave sooner.

Continuing Recovery and Some Scary News   13

February 9 – We travel home. The nurse calls and advises Kathy to increase her dose of cyclosporine from 175mg, twice per day, to 200mg, twice per day, and to increase the prednisone from 5mg per day to 20mg per day. She seems to be saying that the enzymes were elevated and this would help reduce this.

Dr. R calls later, and says that *Kathy may be rejecting her liver*. This is a hit in the gut. We had not heard anything like this on the previous day during our appointment. Her AST and ALT levels had been normal at between 20 and 30 for several weeks, but had suddenly jumped to 64 and 61, or twice normal and slightly above normal, respectively. He said "She's not at 500 on her AST", the intimation being that this is not a major problem, as yet. He says that if her body is healthy enough to recognize a foreign liver, that's a good sign.

Somehow we're not comforted by his words. The higher AST and ALT are indicators of potential onset of rejection, and thus the increased levels of medication the nurse had ordered earlier to avoid this. He also indicates that she doesn't tolerate micophenolate mofetil very well (we know this already from the problems with the deteriorating blood count), and so it's not likely she will take it again. He also says the probability of the CMV virus returning is about 33%.

I ask if we should have any sense of urgency about taking stronger action, and he says no, that we should try the increases in the medication already ordered to see if that works. He would also like to see the cyclosporine level in her blood up to about 250, which is higher than the previously desired range of 150-200, to further reduce the risk of rejection. If the increased dose does not get her enzymes back to normal, then another biopsy will need to be done. If the biopsy indicates she is in rejection, this will require hospitalization and a "pulse" of prednisone of about 500mg, a huge dose. Recall that Kathy had a dose like this once before while in the hospital and when the doctors were concerned about the possibility of rejection.

In the mean time, because of the higher daily prednisone dose of 20mg, we'll have to be more conscious of Kathy's glucose level and the potential for diabetes, as well as higher blood pressure. He also indicates the higher AST/ALT levels could also be caused by an infection or other inflammation in her body, such as what occurred last week when Kathy was sick. We'll just have to wait and see. I keep thinking about the three weeks when her cyclosporine level was near 60 for some unknown reason, and the risk of rejection that goes with that. We're both very worried.

February 10 – We try to return to as normal a life as possible, given the heightened worry about rejection. She slept well last night, in spite of all this.

February 11 – We send a letter to Dr. R, describing our experience with the neutropenia and anemia from January 26 – February 2. The relevant parts are below:

1. **Our Experience.** On January 13, the nurse coordinator advised us to discontinue Kathy's micophenolate mofetil , based on her white count and absolute neutrophils being critically low. We've learned since that she was

neutropenic at the time, a new word for us. Subsequently, her blood count improved for a couple of weeks, but then deteriorated substantially again, and on January 27 the valganciclovir was suspended. At the time my records indicate her hemoglobin was 6.7, and hematocrit was 18.7. She was neutropenic and anemic, and subsequently had four units of blood, two on January 27th, and two on January 29th. As you may know, she was hospitalized at 4:30am on January 28th with a fever, chills, and vomiting, whose cause is still unknown. It could have been 1) a reaction to the transfusion, given that she had already had ~40 units of blood prior to this transfusion and could have benefited from pre-treatment; or 2) an infection, though none of the cultures were ever positive; or 3) a stomach upset; she had a pimento cheese sandwich during the transfusions which contained mayonnaise, something we now avoid in public restaurants. Had we known what neutropenia was on January 13th, we would have taken extra precautions to further minimize the risk of infection, e.g., wearing a mask in all public places. We have also come to understand that when the hemoglobin (Hgb) and hematocrit (Hct) are around 7.5 and 24 respectively, that a transfusion may be in order; and that patients who have had many transfusions may require pre-treatment prior to having additional transfusions.

2. **Our Suggestions**. If not already in place, 1) Establish a protocol to advise post-transplant patients when they become neutropenic, and to take additional precautions when white blood or neutrophil count goes below a certain level; and/or to go to a hematologist for an evaluation and possible treatment with filgrastim. 2) Establish a protocol to advise post-transplant patients to go to a hematologist when the Hgb and/or Hct go below a certain level, e.g., <8 and <24, for a possible transfusion and/or a epoetin alpha shot. 3) Establish a protocol to advise the post-transplant patient that a pre-treatment (acetaminophen, benadryl, steroids) may be necessary prior to any transfusion, given the number of transfusions that the patient has already had. Kathy had some 40 units of blood before, during, and after

the transplant, putting her at greater risk for a transfusion reaction.

Had we known about these things prior to the events of the past month, it would have helped us to mitigate some of them.

I also write a second letter to the Head Floor Nurse of the hospital where Kathy was treated on January 28 – February 2. The relevant points in this letter are repeated below:

The purpose of this letter is to follow up on our conversation while my wife Kathy was a patient at your hospital, as well as my conversation with John (last name unknown) who contacted us shortly after our stay regarding the quality of our stay.

Background

My wife, Mary Kathleen Moore (Kathy), was admitted to your hospital ~4:30am on January 28th having had a fever, chills and vomiting through the night. At the time of admission, she had a fever of 101+, considerably lower than the maximum of 103 that we measured at home at 3:30 am. Fevers are of particular concern to us, since Kathy is a liver transplant patient, and is immune-suppressed from the medications she is taking. On the day prior to her admission, she had two units of blood at the Transfusion Center with only a low grade fever during the transfusions, e.g., 99.5, more or less, but this gradually progressed to something worse into the evening and night.

My understanding is that at the time of admission, she was considered neutropenic, with a very low white blood and neutrophil count, and thus at much greater risk of infection. After contacting the doctor on call at the transplant center, Kathy was admitted and placed on a series of antibiotics to minimize the risk of infection; cultures were taken, and through the course of her stay she was given neupogen and procrit in appropriate doses to stimulate her white and red blood count, among other medications. She was discharged on February 2nd.

The ultimate outcomes from her stay were excellent. The doctors and nurses, as well as support staff seemed very competent and overall caring. However, there were a number of issues that we would like to raise in order to support your continuing effort for improvement, lower the risk to your patients, and provide overall better care and outcomes for all patients at your hospital.

These are provided below.

Our Experience

There were a series of issues that caused us concern during Kathy's stay. These were related to:

1. Laboratory Blood Work
2. Standards for Care of Neutropenic Patients
3. Time Consuming Discharge Process
4. Lab Reports Transmission to Transplant Center

While we discussed the first issue with you while Kathy was in the hospital, and I discussed the second and third issues with John after Kathy's discharge, we thought it appropriate to document our discussion, and raise a fourth issue.

1. **Laboratory Blood Work.** As you know, there were two errors here. On January 29th, the staff withdrew blood from Kathy, but somehow lost or did not complete one of the samples, CBC as I recall, thus requiring a second

sample be taken. On February 2nd, the day of her discharge, a sample was ordered for a CBC, but not taken, requiring a last minute sample prior to discharge. As we discussed, the process seems broken when you have two incidents such as this in a single six-day stay.

2. **Standards for Care of Neutropenic Patients.** Two issues arose here – one general, and the other specific.

    a. General Observations. There was a poster outside Kathy's room providing instructions for persons entering the room, given her condition. It's not clear to me these standards were followed. For example, some of the staff wore masks, but most did not, even those who were in close contact with her checking her IV's, taking her blood pressure, etc. Some wore gloves, but others did not. Some, particularly the cleaning staff, even donned the yellow coveralls along with mask and gloves, but most did not. Some washed their hands before and after working with Kathy, others did not. Kathy was provided with her own blood pressure cuff, but we had to remind several staff members that she had her own cuff, and it was replaced at least twice. All this suggests a need to strengthen the standards in place, to assure that the staff is trained in them, and most importantly, is following them. Perhaps we didn't understand the standards, but it's more likely there is substantial inconsistency in their implementation.

    b. Specific Observation. One of the nurses looking after Kathy kept clearing her throat while attending to her. I asked if she had a cold. She said no, that it was laryngitis. I asked if she should be wearing a mask. She did not respond. This struck me as a more serious thing, since clearly the instructions were if you had a cold or other infection, you MUST wear a mask when in close contact with Kathy. At that point Kathy's neutrophils and total white count were much better, so I did not make a big fuss. But, if a patient is still considered neutropenic, or at risk of returning to that state, the rules must be followed to minimize the risk to the patient.

3. **Time Consuming Discharge Process.** This is more of a major annoyance than a health concern, but it did leave us with one more negative image of your hospital and the discharge process. Dr. A, Infectious Disease, discharged Kathy around 9am; her nurse removed her IV around 11am; at ~11:30 we discovered that her blood had not been drawn to provide a CBC to support her discharge – see above comments; after the CBC was completed, Dr. S3, the Hospitalist, saw her at 2:30, and discharged her; we finally were truly discharged by her nurse at 4:30. It was a long, long day, and something that should have taken an hour or so actually took 7+ hours. This just seems totally out of line.

4. **Lab Reports Transmission to Transplant Center.** On January 31st we stressed to Dr. H5, another hospitalist, the importance of Kathy's blood work including CBC, kidney function, liver panel, and that it was of utmost importance that her cyclosporine level be tested; and that the results of the lab work must be faxed or emailed to the Transplant Center. These tests are performed weekly to check her liver function and anti-rejection medications to assure that there is no rejection and that any other medical concerns that deserve immediate attention are addressed. We stressed this again on Monday, and again on Tuesday. In spite of our repeatedly stressing the importance of getting the lab results transmitted to the Transplant Center, it was not done. When we arrived at the Transplant Center on Monday, February 8th, for a routine checkup, they asked about the blood work for February 1st, since they had not received it. They called the lab that morning and received the information, nearly a week late. So it seems that our repeated requests to assure Kathy's well being through lab results review by the Transplant Center were

ignored. This lack of follow up could have placed Kathy's well being at risk. Fortunately, it did not, but we were very unhappy with this situation.

Summary

As noted in the beginning, all the ultimate outcomes from her stay were excellent. The doctors and nurses, as well as support staff seemed very competent and overall very caring. However, a number of your processes appear broken, particularly with regard to lab work, and in the future could put others in jeopardy. We strongly encourage you to review these issues and take appropriate action to assure excellence in patient care while minimizing risk to the patient.

If you would like to discuss any of the points made in this letter, we would be happy to do so. Or if we've missed or misunderstood anything, we'd be glad to have our understanding corrected. We believe our goals are aligned with yours – the best health care for your patients.

We later received a letter from the hospital indicating that they had addressed all these issues with a number of actions, including re-training, and revision of protocols and procedures. We were very pleased with their response.

February 12-13 – Kathy seems to be tolerating the higher dose of prednisone so far. Her fasting glucose, which was initially at 127 the day after the increased dose of prednisone, has dropped to 101 and 98 over the past two mornings. Dr. R wants her glucose level to stay below 150 and she's well below that. Her post meal levels, when glucose levels naturally rise, have been 135 and 160, also reasonably good considering the amount of prednisone she's taking.
She also seems to have more energy with the added blood and a bit of exercise. She's cooking, walking on the treadmill with me, shopping, doing laundry, etc., though she is pretty tired at the end of the day.

February 14 – It's Valentine's day, and I'm leaving for Germany today on business. I considered postponing it last week, but Kathy says to go ahead, she'll be fine. While I'm not totally re-assured by her assurances, I decide to go ahead. This is another step in trying to get back to normal. It's is my first business trip since last July, and my first trip out of the country since last May, and it's a week long. I'm pretty nervous about it, particularly given the recent news that Kathy's liver may be in rejection.

Liz and Charlie will be coming to stay with Kathy and look after her, which is comforting. Though at this point, she doesn't really need much "looking after". I still worry about the recent episode when she was hospitalized with the high fever, and think it's a good idea to have someone here as a precaution, if nothing else. I'm grateful to Liz and Charlie for their help. And, the doctors don't seem to be overly concerned about the potential for rejection, since the increase in medication may address the problem.

We're grateful to have each other on Valentine's day. We exchange simple cards and an embrace; actually several embraces.

February 15 -19 – I call daily from Germany to check on Kathy and she seems to be doing well. Her blood work tests come back and her AST is slightly better, but her ALT is significantly worse. I get home the evening of the 19th. I'm very relieved to be home. Watchful waiting, and worrying, continues. Is she in rejection?

February 20-21 – We continue to try to live a normal life, doing routine things like cooking, shopping, laundry, house cleaning, visiting with friends, and so on. Of course, we're adhering to her new medication regimen, and getting some exercise.

It's also right about this time that I suggest, or maybe insist would be a better characterization, that Kathy pick up full responsibility for our personal and company books. I had done them while she was so ill, and had helped considerably over the past few weeks since we returned home. I felt she was capable of taking care of these by herself. She was less confident, but I finally persuade her. The next day, I walk into her office, and she's sputtering, and clearly frustrated. As I enter, she lets forth a litany of comments, all of the general tone of "You didn't do this...you didn't enter that...that's not correct...look at this, I told you to enter this data here, and it's not been done," and so on. I'm smiling as she's telling me of all the things I did wrong or didn't do right. She says, rather angrily, "This isn't funny. Now I'm going to have to correct all this." I continue to smile and say simply, "You're baaaack," inflecting my tone as I say it. I give her a hug, and say "Let's have a look. Maybe I can help with fixing my mistakes." She finally relents and hugs me back. It's heart-warming to see Kathy fully engaged in an activity that she used to do routinely. It's another sign of progress.

February 22 – Kathy's blood work comes back for the week, and her AST and ALT are both worse, and significantly above normal at 81 and 161, compared to a normal range of 5-34 and 0-55 respectively. *Dr. R orders yet another biopsy to check for rejection, her third biopsy to check for this.* We're waiting for the coordinator to call and schedule it and are even more worried again. This will be her third post-op biopsy. The prior two did not indicate any rejection. Is this one of those negative "third time's a charm" situations? We hope not.

February 23-27 – We continue to try to live a normal life. No one has called yet to schedule the biopsy and I'm leaving for a project in Colombia on Sunday, the 28th. I'm really very worried about this. We've already contacted Kathy's sister and asked her to stay with Kathy while I'm gone. She will also get Kathy to the Transplant Center for the procedure if necessary, since Kathy is still not comfortable driving, and needs someone there after the procedure.

February 28 – I leave for Colombia today. I'm worried about Kathy, and I feel torn about leaving her. If I knew that the biopsy would be this week, I would postpone the trip. We've been concerned about this for over a month, so I'm assuming that another week's delay won't be a big issue. I'm wrong.

March 1 – It's Monday. I'm in Colombia at this point, and the Transplant Center calls and schedules an appointment for Kathy to have the biopsy on Wednesday, March 3. Why couldn't they have scheduled it earlier, or waited until I got home and do it next week? This is very frustrating.

March 2 – I'm in Colombia and trying to stay focused on the project and taking care of the client. It's very difficult to compartmentalize. I work out in the evenings to try and take some of the worry off my mind.

March 3 – The biopsy is performed today. Now comes the waiting for the test results, which is more nerve wracking.

March 4 – I call Kathy and she has great news. The biopsy is negative, yet again! And, we get a bonus. There's no indication of any return of the autoimmune hepatitis. This is a tremendous relief, and really hard to describe. Elation comes to mind. The doctor reduces her prednisone level from 20mg to 15mg.

March 5-14 – We resume our effort to return to normalcy.

March 15 – We travel to the Transplant Center for Kathy's six-month checkup with Dr. R. It was a beautiful, slightly cool day, so I suggest we go for a walk and then out to dinner. We went for a walk in a local park, a lovely place, and one that we had visited often while Kathy was recovering and we were still living in an apartment near the Transplant Center. There were times then when she could barely walk a hundred yards before being so tired she couldn't go on. Today she easily walks a mile in beautiful sunny weather. It was wonderful, particularly as we reflected on the struggle she had only two or three months ago as she was recovering. I ask her if she ever thought this would be possible again, after having so much difficulty previously. She said "No." We both smile. Here we are enjoying life again.

After our walk we go to dinner, and then she wants to go shopping for a few personal items, though none of these are urgent. I am pretty tired by then, having driven from home, but I was so happy to see her wanting to do things again, we went shopping. I slept well that night. She did too.

March 16 – She has the appointment with Dr. R. He is very pleased with her progress, and essentially all her blood work is normal, including her AST and ALT.

When I ask why the cyclosporine levels in her blood went suddenly within one week from 150 to 60 and stayed that way for three weeks, in spite of increased doses of cyclosporine, he simply says he doesn't know. Likewise, he isn't sure why the AST and ALT levels increased and then went back to normal. Medicine is apparently often a mystery.

There were two measures that were slightly abnormal. Her BUN (blood urea nitrogen, a indicator of kidney function) was a little high, so he encouraged her to drink more water, and her GGT (an indication of bile duct function) was also high, but this could be simply due to the stent in her bile duct slowing the flow of bile. We've been told by Dr. S that until the stent is removed permanently, this will likely continue to be slightly high.

March 17 – After Kathy's six month checkup, I send out what I hope will be our last "status update" on her transplant:

Hi Everybody -

Today is six months after Kathy's liver transplant (a milestone of sorts) and she's doing really well. She had her Six-Month checkup yesterday and her doctor said she's doing great - essentially all her liver, kidney, and blood functions were normal. A couple were a tiny bit high, but trending in the right direction and nothing to worry about. You and I probably have a couple numbers that are slightly high or low at any given time.

She is energetic (though not quite 100% yet), and doing normal everyday things (including fussing at the way I kept the company and personal books while she was sick, so I KNOW she is better - I could only smile when she did this). We arrived into the Transplant Center Monday afternoon for the checkup on Tuesday, and it was a beautiful day, so we walked about a mile in the local park and afterward she was happy to go to dinner and then shopping after dinner - it was just wonderful, particularly considering that it wasn't so long ago that walking 100 yards at this park was a really big effort.

Thank you for all your support, prayers, kind thoughts and best wishes. And, thank you for thinking of and praying for the donor family. We really appreciate that as well. Unless you hear from us directly again, know that she continues to do well. If you know of anyone that needs or has had a transplant and would like to talk with us about our experience (so far), we'd be glad to do anything we can to help.

Our best to all.

March 18-April 6 – It's been a long time (relatively speaking) since my last entry on March 17. I've been to England on a project, but with not nearly as much worry as I've had on previous trips. Of course Liz stayed with Kathy as a precaution and to keep her company. All in all, Kathy has been feeling well. Her blood work has been quite good. The BUN and GGT are still a bit high, but are not of concern at this point; and her ALT is a tiny bit high, but not enough to be concerned about. Her blood count, both her white count and red count, have been normal or near normal for some time now. And, her energy level continues to be good. She's enjoying life again. So am I. As her life goes, so goes mine. We haven't been nearly as worried about her getting a life threatening infection. On Sunday, April 4, we reduce her prednisone from 15mg to 10mg. We expect to go to 5mg the first week of May.

April 7-12 – It's been a busy week and Kathy's energy has been good through it all. We had Jake and Laura over for lunch on Wednesday, then went with friends of ours from Kentucky, Bill and Pauline, to a book review on Cormac McCarthy's works. McCarthy is one of my favorite authors. It's good to know that even the expert (the guy who wrote the book about McCarthy's works) didn't fully understand him and his writing.

On Thursday we go to Kentucky to visit our friends CT and Sherry, and to visit with Bill and Pauline again. From there we go on to Berea College, Kathy's alma mater, for a little shopping and dinner.

On Friday, the 9th, we pick up her Aunt Mary and go to the University of Kentucky for a birthday party for her nephew Zach in the football training facility, where he's a freshman and works as one of the equipment managers, though manager might be too strong a term. We have cake and milk/drinks for all the players. Kathy was even being a mother to some of the players serving cake and milk. She asked one if he wanted milk to go with his cake, and he said "No thank you ma'am." Kathy, who is 5'2", says to this big bruiser of a football player, half playfully and half seriously, "I'm your mother today. You take some milk." He did. We all laughed.

After this we enjoy a visit with other friends from high school who now live in Lexington, Mike and Connie. Finally, we left for home. But, on Saturday morning, the 10th, bright and early, we left for a swim meet in Scottsboro, AL, where Devin, one of our granddaughters was participating. She did well. We also got to see our kids and Devin's brother Andrew. It was a great time. That afternoon we headed back home, stopping to go to church that evening near our home.

On April 11th, we're off to the Transplant Center for a checkup, planning on coming home on Monday, the 12th. When we get there, Kathy wants to do a little shopping, and so we do. Kathy's been in good spirits through all this. Clearly she's feeling better and has a lot more energy for running from pillar to post. I'm tired.

April 13 – Kathy's blood work from the April 12 tests at Transplant Center comes back mostly normal. Her BUN is still a little high (drink more water), but better. Keeping her BUN at a reasonable level will become a continuing struggle. Her GGT is also still a little high, but as noted above, the stent to facilitate bile duct flow can actually constrict and slightly inhibit bile duct function. We continue to strive for normalcy.

April 14-16 – We leave for my mother's in eastern Kentucky to take her to Lexington on Thursday for her routine doctor appointments with the cardiologist and endocrinologist. Those go well – all seems to be normal for someone of her age of 83. She's tolerating her medications well, some of which are new, and is in good spirits. We leave Mom's on Friday to go home, but my brother and his wife, their kids, and the grandkids will be up to see Mom for the weekend. This also keeps Mom in good spirits.

As you can see, with her ability to do all this travel, Kathy's energy is much better. She's enjoying all this, and much more like the "old" Kathy that I had known and loved for so many years, before the liver disease started to take her down.

April 17-23 – We continue to strive for normalcy, but without as much running about. I'm scheduled to go to England on the 20th, but the volcano in Iceland is wreaking havoc with the airlines. My flight is cancelled. We call Liz to let here know that she doesn't need to stay with Kathy. Our daughter, Trish, calls to let us know she's coming for a visit this weekend. We haven't seen them for some time, and a visit will be enjoyable.

Another Crisis 14

April 24 – Little did we know this morning that another crisis is coming. Things have gone well the past few weeks. We've traveled a lot, and Kathy has had excellent energy through it all. We've been cooking and shopping together. The past week has been great. And today, Trish and Carlos and the grandkids are visiting. So, we go to the local Rossini festival with its food, crafts, demonstrations, and singing, including opera. We both love Puccini's Madame Butterfly, which is featured.

However, after we get home from the festival, Kathy is tired and lies down for a nap around 4:30. At 5:30 when I check on her, she has a fever of 99.5, and is aching and chilling, but has no congestion, cough, or headache. I give her two acetaminophen, but her fever still rises to 101. I call the Transplant Center and advise them of her symptoms. They advise that if it goes any higher to take her to the hospital. By 8pm, however it is down to 100.4, and she has less aches and chills, but she is still quite tired. She eats a small meal, takes her meds and goes back to bed. I'm a little encouraged. I recall that yesterday she had diarrhea, and wonder if this could that be related. Could the bacteria or virus causing the diarrhea have migrated into her system?

At 10pm Kathy awakens to go to the toilet and is weak and disoriented. I help her to the toilet. When she gets back to bed, she vomits. Her fever is 102.7. We rush immediately to the emergency room of the hospital. She vomits again on the way there. Her temperature is 103.

She has aphasia, and makes a nonsensical comment. She vomits again in the hospital emergency room. When asking me for something to wipe her mouth after vomiting again, she asks for "liver cottage cheese". It's a very scary moment. We learn later that it is common for patients who have had brain trauma, i.e., brain stem swelling, seizures and brain hemorrhages, to have febrile, or fever induced, encephalopathy and/or aphasia. It appears this is true for Kathy.

They immediately begin a saline IV, take several blood samples, a urine sample, a strep sample, a X-ray, and a CT scan of her chest and abdomen. They contact the Transplant Center and are authorized to give Kathy ibuprofen, something that we've been instructed by the Transplant Center to avoid, apparently because of the potential risk of damage to the kidneys (not the liver). They begin a series of antibiotics as with her last hospitalization in January, that is, piperacillin and tazobactam, vancocin, and levofloxacin, just in case, even though the tests thus far have not indicated any bacterial infection. The ER doctor at one point says rather insensitively "You've got a time bomb on your hands." This does *not* make me feel better. Certainly we understand the risks for Kathy, but "time bomb" seems substantially overstated.

April 25 – Kathy is doing much better by 6:00am. Her temperature is 98.4, and she is literally feeling better. She does not remember vomiting, at home, in the car on the way to the hospital, or at the emergency room. Nor does she remember the aphasia. Her blood pressure (BP) is very low, however, at 75/45, and as a precaution they admit her to the critical care unit (CCU). She is given a dose of steroids to boost her blood pressure. She has breakfast and her normal medications at 8am, except that the 10mg of prednisone is omitted, since she's had the steroids. By 9am, her BP is up to 110/55. She's now reading the paper. The change is remarkable.

We still don't know what caused the illness last night. Her temperature is normal all day and into the evening, but around 9pm her temperature begins to climb again to 99.5. She is chilling and achy as well. She is given a combination of acetaminophen and propoxyphene napsylate for fever and pain, but her temperature continues to rise and by 2am it is 101.5. My anxiety grows, but to my relief it later begins to drop, and the chills and aches dissipate, all with no further medication or action. It all seems a mystery to me.

As with Kathy's last stay in this hospital in January, we insist on controlling the medications related to her transplant, and meet with the doctor to outline our reasoning. After some general discussion, he agrees without hesitation. Again, the hospital handles all medications related to the infection and hospitalization, and the nursing staff is kind enough to remind us about Kathy taking her medications.

April 26 - This morning she is feeling fine and her temperature is normal. The cause of her illness is still a mystery, much the same as it was in January. So far none of the tests have indicated any infection. But, once again the absence of evidence is not the evidence of absence.

April 27 – Kathy continues to feel fine, though her appetite is still not very good. Her temperature and blood work have all come back normal. Dr. A, the same infectious disease specialist that treated her i in January, says it's ok for her to go home. Dr. G, a hospitalist, also says it's ok for her to go home. Their best guess at this point is that she had some form of viral infection that her body fought off by itself, even in its weakened state. However, as a precaution they order a heavy dose of antibiotics in the event that her fever was indeed caused by some unknown bacterial source, and even viral infections can reduce your immune system and make you much more subject to bacterial infection.

We're going home. I'm also happy to report that the hospital did an excellent job this time with following protocols, lab work and discharge. It was a much improved stay.

April 28-30 – Kathy is seriously weakened by the illness, but is recovering and growing stronger. Friday, the 30th is Jake's birthday. She works hard to make sure Jake enjoys his birthday. One of his favorites is chocolate cake and so she spends a lot of time in the kitchen making a meal he will enjoy, especially the cake. Laura, his sister, is also handicapped and they live together along with the help of their caregivers in a home that we purchased for them. Everyone comes to the party. It's a good day.

May 1-3 – While Kathy continues to recover from the illness, she has been having headaches and neck aches over the past few days. And, she's still tired, and is napping as I write this. I'm hoping this is just part of her continuing to recover and nothing more. We need to keep an eye on her blood count numbers. They were depressed from the episode we had over last weekend. In the afternoon she takes another nap, but later we walk on our "dueling" treadmills listening to National Public Radio. She walks a half mile and I'm encouraged by this.

Later in the afternoon, we get a call from the Assisted Living Facility – Kathy's mom, Helen, has aspirated some food and they're bringing her to the ER. I'm off to the ER to bring her medical cards and check on her. Liz and Charlie are there as well. Helen has already had a small lump of meat removed from her throat. After getting a reasonable prognosis, I go home to Kathy, but Liz and Charlie stay with her mother. Over the course of the next few hours the doctors remove another chunk of meat from her throat, and finally she returns to the Assisted Living Facility.

Another crisis has passed, though for Kathy's mother this time. Sometimes it can be trying to deal with a mother in assisted living, make sure our two handicapped kids are being well cared for, help Kathy recover, and still keep up with everything else.

May 4-9 – Kathy has been routinely waking up with a headache. She typically takes an acetaminophen. And, she's more jittery and her trembling has gotten worse. We're somewhat concerned, but she'll be going to the Transplant Center on Monday, May 10th, for an ERCP and bloodwork. That may shed some light on the situation.

May 10 – Kathy's cyclosporine is 509, a very high number, and the likely cause of her headaches and increased jitteriness and increased trembling. It's a toxic level. The Transplant Center currently wants it to be around 250. She's instructed to not take her cyclosporine medication that evening and to reduce the dose to 200 mg, twice per day. During the ERCP that afternoon, Dr. D places two stents in her bile duct. He indicates that this is not unusual and we should not be worried. When I ask if this will be the last time for a stent, he says "No, she'll likely need one stent next time and that should be the last time." This would take her into the nominal one year period that the Green Book indicated a stent is commonly required.

May 11 – We travel home uneventfully, save stopping at a farmer's market where we buy lots of fresh vegetables, something Kathy now wants to eat more of. She's essentially given up fast food at this point, and is moving quickly toward a heart healthy diet. The Transplant Center nurse calls that afternoon to let us know that Kathy's cyclosporine level is 291, much closer to the target level, and below the toxic level of 500+. We're both relieved.

The doctors can't offer any explanation as to why it would suddenly jump to 500+ when we've been on the same regimen, any more than they could offer any explanation for why it dropped to 60 for three weeks back in January on nearly the same daily dose. More experience and learning.

May 12-16 – These are mostly normal days doing routine things. We travel to Kentucky and my mother's on Friday, 14th, to take her to a country and gospel music performance. On Saturday Kathy and I have a small spat over whether she's drinking enough water/liquid. She insists she is, but I tell her that the blood urea nitrogen (BUN) numbers suggest otherwise, and I measure her consumption. I observe that she pours a lot of liquid, but leaves much of it sitting. Pouring is not the same as drinking. We make up very quickly, and enjoy the rest of the weekend. Her blood pressure is up some on Sunday evening to 150/95 and we're somewhat concerned about that.

May 17 – At 5am Kathy's blood pressure shoots up to 177/112, a cause of real concern, especially in light of her previous problems with brain hemorrhages and swelling, and the risk presented to her liver's varices. After notifying the Transplant Center by email, we decide on our own to put her back on a low dose of the blood pressure medications amlodipine (5mg) and metoprolol (50mg). The Transplant Center advises us to contact our local doctor. Though logical, this is not very satisfying. They put her on the blood pressure meds and authorized her to be off. One of the side effects of the other transplant medications can be hypertension, so it seems appropriate they be involved in the decision of what to do. This brings it down some after an hour or so to 145/95 where it stays until mid-afternoon when it drops to 125/85. We relax, some.

May 18 – Kathy's blood pressure is normal in the morning at 120/80, and that evening is 107/67, low, even without any further medications. This is a real mystery. Just 36 hours earlier it was very high and with very limited medication it's now below normal. She stays busy with me during the day cleaning out the kitchen cabinets, and walks that evening.

We receive the results of her blood work on Monday and it's essentially all good, except for her BUN again, which is still slightly high. Her GGT is also slightly high, but it's been that way for months. The doctors are not concerned. One worry is that her cyclosporine level is 376, still quite a bit higher than the targeted level of about 250. The dose is reduced to 175mg, twice per day. She's tired at the end of the day.

Continuing Adjustments

15

May 19-20 – These are good days. We do a little gardening, though Kathy is not allowed to touch the soil, given the risk of infection; some work on the company books; and some general catching up with chores. We enjoy each other's company. On Thursday night, the 20th, we go to our niece Jessica's graduation. It's a very nice event, with really good speakers, which strikes me as unusual. Often these speakers can be pretty boring. And, they had several members of the class sing. They were really good. And, of course, there was the calling of the names of the graduates to receive their diploma. Of course, as each name was called, there seemed to be a group somewhere in the crowd giving a yell for their special graduate. We did as well, giving a yell for Jessica as she received her diploma. It was a good time.

May 21 – I leave for Australia and New Zealand today on business, something that I've done many times before. But, these departures continue to be difficult for both of us. I will be gone for more than two weeks. It's my first really long trip from home. Her sister Julia and her husband Greg are coming to help for the first week, and then Liz and Charlie, will be around to help as needed the second week. We hold one another for long periods this morning. It's a sweet sorrow that we share. We will miss each other terribly, but we know that we must continue to build a normal life, which includes me working, and her carrying on while I'm gone. I believe she can handle this just fine, particularly with her sisters here. But, it won't stop me missing her.

May 22 - June 5 – During this period I'm traveling extensively in Australia and New Zealand – arriving into Melbourne, then to Brisbane, then to Gladstone, back to Brisbane, then to Canberra, back to Sydney, then to Auckland, New Zealand, then finally home. It's a schedule from hell, but the time goes by pretty quickly, and I don't have too much time to brood over missing and worrying about Kathy. We talk daily and that helps some, but it's not like being with her. She seems in good spirits when I call and is doing well. Her cyclosporine level has dropped from 509 to 153 over the past three weeks, even though the dose has only dropped from 225mg twice daily to 175mg twice daily. This is a 300%+ variation in blood level with only a nominal 25% variation in dose.

As noted, the doctors don't seem to know why this happens. She's not done anything that we know to induce such high variation. She's very disciplined about taking the medications at exactly 12 hours apart. We've not changed brands of cyclosporine. She's avoided any foods that are off-limits, like grapefruit, since they can interfere with drug absorption. Anyway, I'm looking forward to getting home. It will be nice to just hold her. She has an appointment with Dr. R on Tuesday, so we can ask questions about her overall health, including the questions about the medications varying so much.

June 6 – It's great to be home. Kathy's doing well. It's nice to be able to hold her, have coffee and read the paper with her, and just have an ordinary conversation about mundane things.

June 7 – We're on our way to the Transplant Center for Kathy's nine month checkup. *Nine months*, one day at a time. We drive leisurely there, stopping several times, for a toilet break, for lunch, to get an ice cream.

That evening we have dinner with Tim and Mary, who were so kind to us just after Kathy's surgery. As you may recall, we had dinner at their home last November. At the time it was our first night out in over a year. It was a wonderful evening then, with lots of joking and pleasant conversation. This evening is no different, as we continue to work on getting back to a normal life.

June 8 – Kathy has Blood work this morning, and an appointment with Dr. R in the afternoon. At the appointment he says she is doing well. All systems are normal, at least normal for a person who's had a liver transplant. We have several questions. Among other things, he advises us that Kathy will not likely need to be on micophenolate mofetil or valganciclovir again. Recall that these are the medications that induced severe anemia and leukopenia. At her one year checkup, she will likely be taken off the antibiotic sulfamethoxazole and trimethoprim, and off ursodiol. She will likely be on cyclosporine, prednisone, and azathioprine, her three anti-rejection medications, forever. He tells us that she may take ibuprofen for no more than two days to help reduce a fever, but generally it is to be avoided due to the risk of damage to her kidneys.

He also advises that it's ok for Kathy to travel overseas for a week or so, but she should have blood work done prior to departure and on her return, and eat only cooked foods to minimize the risk of infection. She should also avoid cats because of they pose a higher risk of infection with more dangerous diseases. Being in a home with dogs is ok, but strictly avoid having them lick or bite, and it's important to wash your hands after petting a dog.

He also advises that blood levels of cyclosporine can vary widely, even with a narrow variation in daily dose, as Kathy has experienced. So, her experience is not out of the ordinary. He does not know why this happens, but it seems common with this particular medication. He also indicates that the reason for the increase in targeted blood level of cyclosporine from ~150 initially to ~250 today is that her immune system is growing stronger, and the higher dose will help minimize the risk of rejection. He also says she can get new glasses at this point. Some of the medications, like prednisone, can affect your vision, and so waiting until that effect has settled down is a good idea to prevent having to get glasses more than one time in a short period. Finally, Kathy can go back to having blood work done every two weeks for now, instead of weekly. It's an indication of progress in my mind.

June 9-13 – We travel home on the 9th, having an uneventful trip. The next few days are also uneventful as we do normal, simple, everyday things, enjoying each other's company.

June 14-16 – Kathy travels with me for the first time since the transplant to a work event. A client has asked me to speak at their company conference on manufacturing excellence. It's in Atlanta, and so Kathy decides to join me. It's really nice to have her travel with me, and to be there for the breakfast and dinner meals, and to spend the evening together. Those are typically pretty lonesome by myself, even if I'm "out with the guys". No doubt, they are also lonesome times for Kathy. It's also good to see her going out independently to do things on her own while I'm working. Doing normal things like this is great.

June 21 – All things have been fairly normal for the past few days. This morning we go for blood work at the laboratory. Unfortunately, the technician that normally does the work is absent, and so a substitute is there.

She arrives late, smelling of smoke, then can't find the orders for Kathy's blood work, and has difficulty getting the laboratory computer to start up. I tell the technician at least three times that Kathy needs a complete blood count for red and white cells, a test for liver function and kidney function, as well as cyclosporine level and GGT. She finally finds what she thinks are the orders and gets the samples needed. Or so we thought. More on that later.

I leave for England this afternoon. Kathy is going to stay home *alone*. This is the first time she has done this in well over a year. Up to now, when I've traveled overseas she's had one of her sisters stay with her, just in case. Now she says she's up to taking care of herself, by herself. This is progress, but makes me a little nervous. I reckon I'm just a worry wart.

One of my final statements to her before leaving for the airport is "You make sure you take care of you first!" A major concern that I have is that the two previous crises we had, where she had a fever of 103F, she developed febrile encephalopathy, the fever-induced period of significant confusion. Moreover, the fever came on quickly, going from normal to 103 F in a matter of a few hours. She promises me that if she has any hint of chills, aches, or fever, that she will immediately get help from her sisters, friends, or neighbors, while she still has her mental capability.

June 22-25 – A complicating issue during my absence is that her mother, who is nearly 88, has taken a turn for the worse including a bout of encephalopathy and aphasia, and is hospitalized. Kathy seems to be taking it in stride.

She spends time with her mother in the hospital and talking with the doctors. After a few days to adjust her mother's medications, she is discharged to the assisted living center.

On Thursday we received the results of the blood work done on Monday, BUT, part of the white count is missing, and the liver function test was not done. A screening for hepatitis A and B was done, but that is something that was not necessary, or ordered. This is in spite of my repeatedly telling the technician on Monday what tests were needed. Clearly, she was not paying attention to the work at hand. This is not surprising given the circumstance at the time of the blood draw. She arrived late, had difficulty finding Kathy's orders, and couldn't get the computer up in a timely manner. The next time we have a substitute, I will ask her to repeat back to me the tests that she is doing, just to be sure. It's another lesson we've learned.

June 26-30 – It's mostly uneventful as we do normal everyday things.

July 1 – For the first time since her transplant, Kathy says "I think I'm getting better." She had been sniffling, so I thought she was referring to getting rid of the sniffles. "No", she says, "I mean I'm starting to feel more like my old self." Finally, years into the disease, and more than 9 months after the transplant surgery, she's beginning to actually feel like her old self.

July 2 – We travel to Kentucky to see our good friends Bill and Pauline. Pauline has recently had open heart surgery to repair two heart valves about two weeks ago. Kathy prepared a simple meal of lentil soup and bread to bring with us. Having been through a similar period after major surgery, she knew Pauline would not feel up to a big meal. It's really good to see Kathy looking after someone else. This is another first in our journey back to normal.

July 3 – We continue on that afternoon to attend a wedding, also in Kentucky. Kathy reads most of the way there, another pastime she is now doing more and more, further confirming that she is "getting better", and returning to her old self.

The wedding is for the son of an old friend from high school, and is near my mother's, so we stay with her, in the home where I grew up. We have another first at the wedding by dancing, first the jitterbug and then the two-step. This is the *first time in years we have danced.* We both see lots of people we hadn't seen in years – old high school classmates, relatives and friends. It was all great!

July 4 – We attend a play with Mom near home. It was really funny. We enjoyed Mom's company over the weekend as well. It's been a great weekend.

July 5-13 – We have an uneventful trip home. The next few days are fairly normal or routine days. We shop and cook more together. She is walking about a half mile to one mile a day on the treadmill, along with all the busy day to day activities. She even has the energy to go to our handicapped kids' house and do some housekeeping and chores. While she's really tuckered out at the end of the day, it represents yet another milestone in her recovery – she actually wants to do some heavy-duty housework!

July 14 – We receive the results of the lab work done on July 6th. I'm concerned about Kathy's kidney function. Her BUN, an indication of kidney function has been slightly high for months, so this isn't unusual, but her creatinine, also a measure of kidney function is now also slightly higher, when it had been normal, and her GFR, yet another measure of kidney function has also deteriorated. I send an email to the Transplant Center asking them to review this and for any instructions they might provide.

July 15-21 – These are pretty normal days doing routine things. I've had no reply from the Transplant Center regarding my question on Kathy's creatinine and GFR. On the 19th we go for Kathy's bi-weekly blood work.

July 22-27 – We leave on the 22nd for Washington, DC, where Ken and Joanne live, along with their five children. Joanne is also "with child", so we'll be adding another grandchild to the list in the fall. We haven't been to their home since they moved from Atlanta last year, so we're looking forward to it. They're both West Point graduates, and Joanne is serving at the Pentagon. Ken resigned his commission several years ago, so he could be with Joanne who was pregnant with their first child. He works out of their home for a large data processing company, also serving as "Mr. Mom" as required. On Monday, we'll also be doing a tour of DC with my business partner from England and his family. They're on "holiday" as it's called in England, and DC is on their itinerary. We're looking forward to seeing everyone.

The trip is great, except for the 100F weather, which could be stifling at times. We enjoy our visit with Ken and Joanne, and especially the grandkids. They are all, save the youngest, excellent swimmers and swim competitively, and we go to a meet where they do really well. One of them, Jack, has recently broken a 10 year record in his region by some three seconds, and he's at the younger end of his age group.

Later, we go to a movie and then to the Smithsonian Air and Space Museum, and just generally enjoy the time with each other. Monday, the 26th is also very nice, as we tour the capitol with our friends from England. The trip home on the 27th is uneventful, except for the traffic in DC which is quite burdensome.

July 28-29 – The 27th was Kathy's mom's birthday, but we were unable to celebrate it since we were traveling home, so the 28th is the big celebration. Julia is up from Florida and we, along with her sister's Liz and Lanie, as well as other family members, have a party at the assisted living center. We even repeat this on the 29th, though with a smaller group. A good time was had by all on both days. We continue to work toward a normal life.

July 30 – We bring Julia to the airport to return to Florida. This is always a sad moment, especially for Kathy, who is very close to her sisters, but no doubt Julia will be happy to get back to her husband.

August 1-2 – The day is pretty uneventful until Ken and Joanne arrive the evening of the 1st with the five grandkids to spend the night with us on the way to his sisters in Alabama. It's always a pleasure to have them. We enjoy visiting with the grandkids. It's pretty hectic when you go from two in the house to nine. This is twice we've seen them in one week, after not having visited since Thanksgiving. It's great.

August 3 – We have an appointment with Dr. S, and he's happy with Kathy's progress. However, on review of her lipid panel, he notes that her cholesterol is high at 275 (<200 is preferred), and her triglycerides are also high at 240 (<150 is preferred). So, he advises her to minimize saturated fats (she is already, being on a heart healthy diet), to minimize high glycemic index foods, like sweets and low fiber carbs, and to begin taking fish oil for its Omega 3, 6, and 9, along with flax seed oil, to see if those will help reduce her overall cholesterol level and increase the good cholesterol, so-called HDL.

On reviewing her kidney function tests, he cautions her not to get dehydrated and not to let her blood pressure get low, that is, keep it normal, to assure good profusion of the kidneys. We leave his office and immediately go to the health good store for the supplements and begin taking them that evening. I do as well. It won't hurt me and might even help.

We travel to Huntsville that afternoon to visit with most all the kids and grandkids (9 of the 12) and have one huge party (Ken and his family have traveled to Huntsville, where two of our daughters live). It's great that Kathy can routinely do this kind of family visiting. I think of the past 18 months and how little we could enjoy our family. I'm very grateful for this return to normalcy.

Another concern arises that evening. We get an email from the Transplant Center stating that Kathy's BUN and creatinine continue to be elevated, and have recently risen even more. They advise her *again* to drink more water, a minimum of two liters per day, and preferably three. If these numbers don't return to normal, her kidneys will be damaged. Her condition indicates non-intrinsic kidney disease, likely induced by the cyclosporine. It is common for the medications to induce problems elsewhere, in this case the kidneys, and so they may have to reduce her cyclosporine dose to avoid damage to them. But, a lower cyclosporine dose increases the risk of rejection. It's a constant struggle to balance all the requirements. Kathy pours a lot of liquids, like water and tea, but much of it is left in half empty glasses. This is something I have admonished her about a number of times and so we discuss how we can better manage this.

August 4 – We begin to keep a log to accurately measure and record Kathy's daily fluid intake, much the same as we measured her exact intake of protein before the transplant. She decides to extend this to include protein, fat, carbohydrates, and calories, much the same as we were doing before her transplant to assure minimum nutrition. Only this time it's to assure that she's on a diet that minimizes high glycemic index foods to help lower her triglycerides and "bad" fats, like saturated and trans-fats.

August 5-12 – These are pretty ordinary days, doing routine things. I like ordinary, very much. Her fluid intake is running at a minimum of two liters per day.

August 13 – I leave for Australia today on business. We're both a bit nervous this time. She will be spending the time that I'm gone *alone again*, but this time for more than two weeks, her longest time alone since the transplant. Despite the loneliness, she's more comfortable being alone now. Further, Liz is having surgery next week. So, *Kathy may be going from cared-for to caregiver*, a turnabout for sure, and a clear sign of her progress. I should be encouraged by this, but I'm ever the worry wart about everything proceeding smoothly. We've had too many setbacks and crises in the past. In any event, here we go into another phase of our new lives.

August 15-27 – Traveling to Australia, you cross the international dateline, and essentially lose a day, so I've missed August 14th. While I'm gone Kathy gets her blood work done, and the Transplant Center advises her to keep her medications the same. Her BUN and creatinine are both somewhat better with her increased liquid consumption, but still not normal. With that in mind, they advise her to consume a *minimum* of three liters of water/liquid per day.

This is very difficult for Kathy to do. It's about 24-8oz glasses per day, and it induces a lot of trips to the bathroom. Sleep comes in short periods. I begin to worry about her sodium level being reduced. It's one more adjustment to make. While I'm gone, I call her twice a day just to see how she's doing.

August 28 – It's nearly midnight when I finally get home today. It's good to hold Kathy again. Out of a sense of caution, we've started a practice of not kissing for at least three days after my return. Being in foreign countries for several days at a time, and in planes for hours on end, likely exposes me to any number of diseases. So, as a precaution we've begun this practice to minimize the risk of her being exposed to diseases. The thought being that if I'm infected, it should show up in me within three days of my return.

August 30 – Kathy has a mammogram and pap smear test today. These are now mandatory for her. She's been doing this for years, so this isn't really a change for her. At her age it's just good practice. In the afternoon we make our way to the Transplant Center. Kathy will have her one-year checkup with Dr. R tomorrow at the Transplant Center. *One Year, another milestone!* To be accurate, it's a couple weeks short of a year, but since she's having the stent in her bile duct replaced, the Transplant Center agreed to combine the appointments.

August 31 – Kathy has her blood work done and then an appointment with a physician's assistant to Dr. R. Though it seems less than ideal, it is pretty common to see the PA, unless there is some cause for concern and the doctor *must* see her. All goes well with the appointment. The PA advises that she won't need to come back for one year, that she can discontinue an antibiotic she's been taking for the past year, and that her 5mg daily dose of prednisone will likely be reduced to 2.5mg. This all represents continuing progress.

In the afternoon, Dr. D does the ERCP and puts three stents in place to facilitate bile duct flow. This is a disappointment. We had hoped her bile duct would be sufficiently healed and open so that no further stents would be necessary at all. She had a single stent for the first six months after the surgery, and then in June went to two stents, and now three. Dr. D says he is trying to avoid Kathy needing surgery to repair the bile duct. So, he dilated the bile duct even more than normal, and put in the three stents. While a disappointment, we both reckon it's better than major surgery.

Later in the afternoon the Transplant Center calls to tell us to continue with the present dose of medications, and that she can go to having blood work done every four weeks instead of every two weeks. However, her BUN and creatinine, both indications of kidney function, are elevated again to 43 and 1.5 respectively. They again encourage her to drink more water/liquid to keep her kidneys better hydrated, preferably three liters per day. I respond that because of the ERCP she hadn't had any liquid since 8pm the night before, so this might be contributing to the elevated levels, and ask if we should have her blood checked again in two weeks. No, just drink more water is the reply.

September 1 – We travel home today from the Transplant Center. It's uneventful, save stopping at the Farmer's Market for some fresh fruit and vegetables.

September 2 – Today is our wedding anniversary. Given the events of the past year or so, I'm simply glad that she is here to celebrate it. It's really difficult to describe my feelings. I get her flowers and a mushy card. We go to dinner in the evening to celebrate. Nice.

September 3-5 – It's Labor Day weekend. We have Jake and Laura for lunch on Friday, and they're in fine spirits. It's a good visit. In the afternoon, we're off to Mom's for the Scott Family reunion for her side of the family. Being the oldest of the 13 siblings in her family, Mom is a bit of a family matriarch, with all the good and not-so-good that goes with that.

It's a pleasant weekend, catching up with relatives and renewing friendships. Kathy continues to be cautious about getting any infections, especially among large crowds like this. She regularly uses her hand cleaner, microwaves the buffet food to a higher temperature, avoids people who are coughing, or seem ill, and so on. It does add an element of work and mild concern that we just have to live with. The alternative would be not to attend these kinds of gatherings, something we both agree would limit our lives too much. The trip home is uneventful.

September 6 – Today is quiet, a rest day. We have a lazy morning drinking coffee and reading the paper. Later today we plan to go to a movie.

September 7-14 – Mostly normal days doing routine things. Kathy is up to walking a mile a day. We receive the results of her lipid panel done on August 31, and her cholesterol is up to 307, in spite of taking fish oil and flax seed oil every day for the past month.

We'll be seeing Kathy's gastroenterologist in the next month or two, and he may put her on statins, which are typically not good for the liver. It seems her new liver is really good at producing cholesterol.

September 15 – We have an appointment with Dr. H3, a nephrologist, or kidney specialist. Kathy's creatinine and BUN level, indicators of kidney function has been climbing over past several months, creatinine going from 0.8 to a high of 1.5, a major change in just a few months. Normal is 0.8 to 1.2. The Transplant Center has advised her to drink more water, three liters per day, and has indicated that they may reduce her dose of cyclosporine to minimize the risk to her kidneys. Of course, a lower dose of cyclosporine likely increases the risk of rejection. So, as a precaution we've decided to check with a kidney specialist to see if there are other things we need to be doing.

Dr. H3 indicates that drinking three liters of water will not likely do any good, and that two liters or less per day will be sufficient. This is inconsistent with the Transplant Center's instructions, so we need to resolve it. He's glad to hear that we've discontinuing the antibiotic she was on, which he says can also have a negative effect on the kidneys.

He observes that her creatinine has increased from about 0.8 to a high of 1.5 over the course of about six months, which is concerning to him. He wants to make sure there is nothing else wrong with the kidneys, and so orders a series of tests – UA, Urine C/S, CBC, CMP, PO4, Mg, and uric acid, along with ANA, C3, C4, and a 24 hour urine for protein immunofixation, and a kidney ultrasound. We will see him again in two weeks for the results of these tests.

He also indicates that her blood pressure was a bit high when he took it, and this can have a negative impact on her kidneys. He asks us to monitor it twice daily, something we're already doing, and report back to him. We advise him that it hasn't been a problem, and that she may be nervous about seeing yet another doctor.

September 16 – *We get our annual flu shot. This is really important*, given the immune-suppressed state that Kathy is in. Other than this, it's an ordinary day.

One Year, and Counting

16

September 17 – *This is the one year anniversary of her transplant surgery.* She's made it through the first year, the highest risk period. We're cautiously encouraged, and continue to look forward to our lives together working hard to make it as normal as possible. We have Jake and Laura over for lunch, and to celebrate Laura's birthday, a couple of days early. She's enthused with all the attention.

September 18-19 – Ordinary days, working around the house. Kathy begins collecting urine on the 19th for the 24-hour kidney function test.

September 20 – We bring her 24-hour sample to the labs the first thing in the morning. I'm leaving for England today, and as usual, we're both a bit sad to see that happening. I have increasing confidence in her ability to take care of herself in my absence, but it's less of a worry since this is a short trip. I'll be home on the 23rd. She seems to be in good spirits while I was gone. Her kidney function continues to be a worry.

September 24-25 – Ordinary days, except for one important event. Catherine Bridget Moore, our 14th grandchild was born on the 25th. As always, it's wonderful news. Baby and Mom, Joanne, are doing well. We go to Mass that evening and give thanks for this blessing. I also say a brief prayer for all our grandchildren, including one, Andrew Charles Robinson, that passed away after being with us for only two months, dying of sudden infant death syndrome.

September 26 – An ordinary day. We go shopping and to a movie. I actually enjoy shopping with Kathy now.

September 27 – Kathy goes in for blood work for the first time in four weeks. We'll see how this comes out and whether or not they order a reduction in the cyclosporine. I call my son Ken to wish him a happy birthday.

September 28 – I attend a local conference on manufacturing practices. It's a good conference with several good presentations on practices and principles.

September 29 – Kathy and I go to see Dr. H3, her nephrologist, who has the results of the tests and mostly good news. The ultrasound indicates no hydronephrosis, no mass or calculus, and no aortic aneurysm; her blood count is essentially normal, except, as usual, her BUN and creatinine are elevated at 35 and 1.37, and both are known side effects of the cyclosporine. Her creatinine is slightly improved from the last test of 1.5. But, now there's a new problem, with her uric acid elevated at 7.2, versus a normal range of 2.4 to 5.7. This is consistent with the high BUN level. Her blood pressure is within the normal range, and so he is not worried about this anymore.

Out of all this, he orders a daily dose of 100mg of allopurinol to help reduce her uric acid level and to better control her BUN/creatinine. This is the lowest dose in a range of 100-800mg.

While checking into the side effects of this medication, I find that it has rare, but serious side effects, especially when taken with azothioprine. This combination can simultaneously lower your red and white blood count, called pancytopenia, induce severe skin rashes, and in fact, induce hepatitis, or inflammation of the liver, something we must avoid.

Later in the day we receive an email from the Transplant Center that Kathy's blood work is ok, and no changes in medications are necessary. Incidentally, her creatinine is 1.19 at this point, in the normal range for her, but her BUN is still high at 37, though better than the previous reading of 43. Maybe drinking more water is working.

September 30 – We travel to our friends in Kentucky for a lobster feast. These are friends that we had been visiting in Maine for many years, but with recent illnesses, both Kathy's disease and CT's kidney disease, we have missed our annual lobster dinner in Maine. So we decide to have it in Kentucky. We get the lobster at a local supermarket, lobster and crab bisque from a local restaurant, corn on the cob, and all the fixings and traveled there for the feast. It was great to celebrate all the good memories with good friends and food.

October 1 – Kathy and I have a discussion about the orders of Dr. H3 and given our concern about the side effects of the allopurinol, we send a letter to the Transplant Center, details of which are below:

> Because Kathy's creatinine and BUN have increased steadily over the past 9 months (see attached plot of creatinine/BUN vs. time), we saw a local nephrologist on September 15, Dr. H3. He was quite concerned about the rise in her creatinine levels, but admittedly has little experience with liver transplant patients. In any event, to make sure that there was nothing developing beyond the effect of the cyclosporine and other medications, he ordered a series of tests that day – UA, Urine C/S, CBC, LMP, PO4, Mg, Uric Acid, 24-hour Urine for Protein Immunofixation, ANA, C3, and C4, and an ultrasound of her kidneys and bladder. Those results are also attached, fyi.
>
> Summarizing all this, most all the results were normal, except for, as you might expect, BUN (35), EGFR (39), Creatinine (1.37), and Uric Acid (7.2). The ultrasound was generally negative/normal – no hydronephrosis, no mass or calculus, no aneurysm, and only a mild plaque in the aorta. In the most recent labs on September 27, and that you have, Bun was 37, Creatinine 1.19, and EGFR was 46.

Based on the results of the tests on the 15th, he has recommended/ordered the following:

1. Medication to reduce uric acid (and risk of gout/kidney stones)– Allopurinol, 100mg daily
2. Biopsy of Kidneys to baseline current condition.

Before we proceed with these, we wanted to clear it with Dr. R. Though reported as rare in all instances, allopurinol when used with azathioprine (one of Kathy's meds) can induce pancytopenia; can induce severe skin rashes; and can induce hepatitis. Dr. H3 is happy to discuss these results and recommendations with Dr. R, and is happy to have CMC do the biopsy, if you think it's necessary. Kathy and I are also happy to come and see Dr. R to discuss the results of these tests, or whatever you may recommend. Note that we're scheduled to come back to CMC in late November/early December for yet another stent replacement, so we could see Dr. R then if necessary.

Could you please provide this information to Dr. R and advise us? We're ok with charging for this consultation as well, even if not covered by our insurance. Thanks for your help in advance.

Ron (and Kathy)

Dr. R responded later that day indicating that he had no problem with Kathy taking the low dose of allopurinol, subject to more frequent blood work to check for these known side effects, particularly the pancytopenia, but that he saw no benefit in doing the biopsy. He also indicated he would be happy to see us in December when we return for the stent replacement; and to talk with Dr. H3 at his convenience.

After talking with Kathy, we advise Dr. H3 that we will begin the allopurinol on my return from Australia on October 25, but will delay the kidney biopsy for now. Given all the potential serious side effects, Kathy doesn't want to start the medication until my return.

October 2-7 – These are ordinary fall weekend days, with college football, a movie, housekeeping, church, shopping, laundry, office work, and the like. Kathy continues to walk a mile or so a day. Incidentally this is at a 5% grade, which is pretty steep. I attend a local conference where I'm an invited panel member offering an opinion regarding the issue of replacing an aging workforce. My primary qualification is being among the aging.

October 8-22 – I leave for Australia today for two weeks on business. Kathy goes with me to the airport, but she's going to her sister's in Florida for a week. She enjoys visiting with her sister, and it helps her pass the time while I'm gone. We talk daily while I'm in Australia, sometimes twice a day. The ability to do this illustrates that even from the most remote corners of the world, like the Pilbara region of Australia, you're never more than a phone call away. For me, Kathy is never more than a thought away. While she's in Florida, her blood pressure is normal, but on returning home, but while I'm still gone, her blood pressure climbs to around 140/90, more or less. She speculates that she's nervous about living alone.

October 23 – I get home late this evening from Australia. It's a bear of a trip, and I'm really tired. My daughter, her husband and two kids came in last night for a college football game. We have a really pleasant visit with them. Kathy is clearly returning to her normal self, having the energy to be the loving "Nanna" that the grandkids have known in the past.

October 24 – Kathy's blood pressure returns to near normal at 130/85. Kathy's Aunt Betty, a favorite, is hospitalized late today with what we learn later is a heart attack and the doctors seem quite concerned. Kathy's mother, who is in an assisted living facility, becomes very agitated because we won't immediately bring her to see her sister. Kathy and I go to the hospital to see how Aunt Betty is doing and to anticipate bringing Kathy's mother to see her. When I call to arrange a time for Helen to visit Aunt Betty, she becomes even more upset because we didn't bring her with us. She hangs up on me. Being sandwiched in between a transplant patient and a really elderly mother can be difficult at times.

October 25 – A pretty ordinary day, save dealing with Kathy's mother's anxiety regarding her sister. We fill the prescription for allopurinol. Kathy's blood pressure returns to ~115/75, not withstanding her mother's anxiety and the tension that results from that. Of course this confirms for Kathy her speculation about the cause of her elevated blood pressure being associated with my absence. I'm still not convinced.

October 26 – Kathy begins the low dose of allopurinol today. We'll be keenly aware of the potential side effects of this and will schedule blood work every two weeks to check for pancytopenia and hepatitis, and be keenly aware of any rashes that develop.

We bring Helen for her doctor's appointment, and then after we go to see Aunt Betty. Helen seems to be doing fine with the visit, until we get back to the assisted living facility, at which point she gets upset with me again, and expresses it in no uncertain terms, for not bringing her to see Aunt Betty sooner. I decide not to engage very much and walk away. Engaging won't help.

October 27-28 – Kathy and I travel to Atlanta where I'm speaking after dinner for one of my clients. We enjoy the trip, and the dinner is really good. One moment was really heart warming. We selected a table up front so I could quickly start my presentation after being introduced. Unfortunately, I had to leave Kathy at the table alone while I was getting everything ready. While I was doing that, someone from another table came and got her and took her to their table. From all appearances she was having a lot of fun at their table. There was lots of laughing, talking and mild boisterousness. It warmed my heart to see Kathy engaged in conversation and laughing with a large group of people. That's the Kathy I've known and loved for years. We traveled toward home that evening, stopping about half way. We arrive home the next morning, about an hour before Jake and Laura arrive for their weekly visit. We have an enjoyable visit.

October 29-November 3 – We travel to Savannah for a long weekend, and then business the next week. It's one of our favorite places and we haven't been here in years. It's pretty much the same and we enjoy just relaxing. On Sunday we travel on to St. Simon's Island, which is very near where I have a small project. It's not often that I have a project near a resort. Save my having to work during the day, we have a very pleasant and relaxing stay here. We particularly enjoy having dinner one evening with Pat, the plant manager, and his significant other, Leslie. Though her stamina still isn't back to where it was pre-transplant, it continues to be good to see her enjoying herself in these kinds of activities.

November 4 – We have an appointment with Dr. S, who continues to be very pleased with Kathy's progress, though her cholesterol level is still a concern at 300+. He suggests a low-carb diet, similar to the Adkins diet. He says it should lower her cholesterol, since carbohydrates tend to stoke the liver's fire for producing cholesterol.

So, here we go again with a new diet. I think we need to do more research on this. Carbs also stoke the body's energy level, and protein and fat are harder to convert to energy. We continue to have some concern regarding Kathy's kidney function and the relationship between the kidney and liver functions, and in particular the impact of the anti-rejection medications. It's not clear what the best course of action is for getting the balance right. And of course her cholesterol level is a concern. Her new liver, though we're extremely grateful for it, is good at making cholesterol, with her levels running near 300. And, this is in spite of a reasonably heart healthy diet, including fish oil and flaxseed oil, which does not seem to have helped.

We schedule an appointment with Dr. R for December 7th, when Kathy has yet another ERCP scheduled to replace or remove the stents in her bile duct. We need some guidance on any appropriate medication for cholesterol control in light of her history, along with guidance on getting the kidney and liver functions properly balanced. We sure don't want to damage this new liver, or her kidneys, or create the conditions for a stroke or heart attack in the future. It continues to be a hard balance to strike.

November 5 – Jake and Laura join us for lunch and we all have a very good day. Jake is full of himself today, having a lot of energy. Laura is very loving and happy.

November 6-8 – Kathy has the sniffles. In the past, this would not have been any worry at all. Now, I'm a bit on edge, considering her history of running a temperature for no known reason, and since any little infection could develop into something deadly. She's feeling a bit better on Monday, when we go to get her blood work done. I relax.

As discussed above, she's on allopurinol now to reduce her uric acid and help with the kidney function. Unfortunately, as we said, when used in combination with one of her other medications, azothioprine, it can cause hepatitis, severe rashes, and lower her white and red blood count. So, we're checking her blood now every two weeks instead of four. And she also had her cholesterol checked, since she's been on a different diet to help with this. We're trying to avoid any new medication, but that may not be possible. We'll see as the time passes.

November 9 – We contact Kathy's dietician, Kayla. We had worked with her prior to Kathy's transplant, and need her advice regarding managing Kathy's cholesterol. She was excellent during Kathy's pre-transplant period, something I am hesitant to say about the Transplant Center dietician, given our experience with encephalopathy induced by a high protein diet, and the low blood sodium induced by the low sodium diet in combination with the aldactone.

Dr. S has suggested something similar to the Adkins diet which has only 40 grams of carbs per day. This may be a problem, since Kathy's glucose levels tend to be on the low end and it hasn't been much more than 100, even an hour after eating breakfast. On her last test it was 64 after breakfast, a pretty low number. She's been on this low-carb diet for a couple days now, and is reporting increased "shakiness" and very low energy. I'm thinking she's not getting enough carbs. We're trying to avoid medications to control the cholesterol, but that may not be possible.

We also want to check on any foods that that might help reduce her uric acid as well. We set up a meeting for early December to see what we can do by using her diet to better manage these issues.

November 10 – *Today Kathy and I received a letter from the mother of the donor, along with pictures of her son, who was only 18 at the time of his death. It's extremely difficult to express the emotion we felt. We both cried silently together as we looked at his pictures and read the letter. We had such mixed feelings of sadness for the death of such a handsome young man, knowing the agonizing heartbreak his mother and father, friends and relatives surely felt; and such gratitude in knowing that Kathy is alive because of him. We know it's small comfort to someone who has lost a child, but we will do our very best to make sure his and his mother's gift is taken good care of, and will live our lives with him always in mind.*

November 11-12 – Kathy has not been feeling well the past few days. She has not had a fever, but is very tired and has had some minor sneezing, coughing and nasal drip. I go back and review the blood work from Monday, November 8th, and notice that although she has not had a significant deterioration in her white and red counts. While they're down slightly, they're within the error band of any given test and not statistically significant as yet. However, her monocytes, a key element in her white count, have dropped dramatically from 7.8 to 2.0.

This gives me some cause for concern, particularly given her tired, cold-like condition. After some thought and discussion, between Kathy and me, and with Charlie and Liz, we decide to suspend her taking allpurinol, since it can have a pretty dramatic effect on her blood count and immune system. This is just one more example of having to keep an eye on everything. I'll get in touch with Dr. H3 about this.

November 13 – I'm on my way to England again for business. Kathy seems to be feeling a little better. As always, I worry about her being alone while I'm gone. And, as always, I miss her.

November 14-21 – The trip to England goes well, but Kathy continues to feel tired and listless, and the mild cold-like symptoms continue to linger. Part of this is likely simply because she is alone, but we're both suspecting that her blood count may be low, since tiredness is a common symptom of low hematocrit and hemoglobin. Since suspending the allopurinol, we had hoped these symptoms would improve, but that doesn't seem to be the case. While she is a tiny bit better, she's still tired.

November 22 – We go in for blood work this morning. Hopefully we'll get some indication from this as to why she's feeling so tired.

November 24 – We get the results from the blood work back today. Her hemoglobin is down some, to 10.2, and her hematocrit is down even more, to 29.9. To some extent this explains her tiredness, and could be the residual effect of the allopurinol.

Her white count is also down, perhaps because of the slight cold she's had. Liz has said that viruses tend to lower your white count, while bacterial infections tend to raise your white count. The blood count numbers are all below normal, but not critically so. We continue with watchful waiting.

November 25-27 – Lots of company and activity around Thanksgiving and the long weekend. Kathy even goes to a football game on Saturday and enjoys the day. We enjoy seeing all the friends and family. She's pretty worn out at the end of it all.

November 28 – It's a Sunday, a rest day after all the activities and festivities. We bring Helen to visit Aunt Betty in the hospital, who asks if we're coming to say goodbye. Though she hasn't been told, it's clear that she knows she's dying.

Aunt Betty blows us a kiss from her hospital bed as we leave. As we will soon know, this will be our final memory of her. It's a wonderful one.

November 29 – I leave today for Iceland. In spite of the sadness of being apart, Kathy seems to be doing fine alone now.

November 30-December 3 – The work in Iceland goes well. Surprisingly, it's actually colder where we live than it is in Reykjavik. We communicate by email, since my phone system doesn't work there. Kathy seems to be doing well during the week, but it's good to get back home on the third.
We have a meeting that afternoon with, Kayla, our dietician. For two hours we review Kathy's status and goals. Her cholesterol continues to be high at around 300; and her uric acid is too high, and could induce gout. Kayla outlines a balanced "Mediterranean" style diet, along with doses of omega-3 through fish oils and flaxseed oil; and a dose of cherry extract to help reduce the uric acid. Kathy has not tolerated the allopurinol very well, with its negative effect on her blood count. We're hoping the combination of extra liquids and the cherry extract will help reduce the impact the cyclosporine is having on her kidneys. Managing all this is a constant effort.

December 4 – *A bad Saturday.* Kathy's aunt passed away this morning, something that we've been expecting, but it's still sad when it happens. We go to Kathy's mother at her assisted living facility to break the news to her. She takes the news about as well as we could expect. They were very close and so we were quite concerned about how she would react. Later Kathy shops for her mother's clothing to wear to the funeral.

December 5 – *A really bad Sunday.* We're on our way out the door to go see Kathy's mother, when the assisted living facility calls. Kathy screams, "NO!" I don't remember what she says after that. Kathy's mother passed away suddenly in the early afternoon. She had not been well for several years, and apparently her heart finally gave out, we think because of the strain of losing her sister. As she was getting up from her chair, she simply collapsed and died. Kathy is in a state of mild shock. I'm very concerned about her and how this will affect her health. After getting over the initial shock, we call the family. Now we have two funerals to attend, one of which we must plan. Kathy also has an ERCP scheduled for Tuesday at the Transplant Center that we have to re-schedule.

December 6 – We're now planning Kathy's mother's funeral, and planning on attending her Aunt's funeral. It's all really difficult to deal with, but Kathy troops on. This evening we attend Aunt Betty's wake. She was a great lady and we feel honored to have been a part of her life. She is in so many fond memories.

December 7 – We attend Aunt Betty's interment, and then that evening we attend Helen's wake. It's all very sad. We have pictures ala a slide show depicting Helen's life, much the same as they had for Aunt Betty last night. It reflects so many good memories at so sad a time.

December 8 – We attend Helen's interment, and immediately travel to the airport to go to the medical center for Kathy's ERCP, re-scheduled for the next day. It's a solemn time.

December 9 – We get some good news, for a change! The doctor removed all three stents and concluded that Kathy did not need any more stents in her bile duct. After the last ERCP, and placing in the three stents, the doctor had indicated that if this doesn't work, she may need corrective surgery. We were quite concerned about this. After being discharged, however, Kathy is very ill. She is chilling and vomiting, but has no fever. I'm on the verge of taking her back to the hospital when, after vomiting for the third time, she begins to feel better. No fever still. She sleeps. I'm relieved.

December 10-12 – We travel to Ashburn, VA, near Washington, DC, where Ken and Joanne, our son and his wife, have a number of activities planned. Their oldest daughter, Nathalie, is being confirmed. Their youngest, Catherine or Cate, is being baptized, and in between there's an "a cappella" choir performance in which he is singing. It's a great weekend, after all the sadness of the previous week.

December 13-19 – We get home at 1am on the morning of the 13th, due to lots of flight delays because of poor weather. After catching a little sleep, we begin the process of handling Helen's estate by contacting various agencies to notify them of her death, contacting the probate court, and so on.

It's a difficult process to go through and forces a bit of re-living her death. Kathy seems to be holding up well. She is however, tired and weak, from the trauma of her mother's death, her aunt's death, the ERCP, and the travel. No doubt it will take a few days for her to regain her strength.

December 20-22 – On Monday, we go for Kathy's bloodwork. On this occasion she's also having her uric acid checked, and a lipid panel done to check her cholesterol and tryglycerides. She's been taking cherry extract now for a couple weeks, and we're hopeful this homeopathic remedy will reduce her uric acid. We're hopeful that the effects of the allopurinol on her blood count have dissipated, and that it's closer to normal.

The Transplant Center also reduced her cyclosporine just slightly from 375mg per day to 350mg to help with reducing her creatinine, BUN, and uric acid levels. And, she's been on a fairly disciplined heart healthy diet, limiting saturated fats to no more than 15g per day, and eating more healthy fats like the mono- and poly-saturated fats found in olive and canola oil and nuts. Kathy finally seems to be re-gaining her strength and energy. She's back to walking a mile, and at a 5% incline. This is really good.

December 23 – Kathy has an appointment with Dr. S, her gastroenterologist. Kathy's latest labs/lipid panel indicate that her cholesterol is still elevated at 288, with an HDL of 34, and and LDL of 190, and perhaps even worse a VLDL of 64. Her triglycerides are 318. These are all bad numbers, and put her at much greater risk of heart disease or stroke. The numbers are still elevated in spite of having taken omega-3 and flaxseed oils the past six months and having been on a low-fat, moderately low-carbohydrate diet for the past three months. We're disappointed with the results.

Dr. S is reluctant to put Kathy on cholesterol reducing medication because of the potential risk to her liver. I make the point that before the Kathy's transplant, she went through a battery of tests, among which it was concluded that she has no significant stenoses in her carotid arteries or heart.

Given that, and the long period over which atherosclerosis develops, and her relatively low risk profile for heart disease (non-smoker, low-stress, not-overweight), I ask if it would be better to live with the problem, rather than risk damaging her liver. We pose this question to the Transplant Center, and they advise that in spite of this, she should go on statins to reduce her cholesterol.

One key negative issue is that her family does have a history of cardiovascular disease. Her mother just died of a heart attack. The logic here is apparently that the risk to her liver with the medication is less than the risk of developing serious cardiovascular disease without it. We've found over the past couple of years, that it's a constant balancing act of managing risk. I forward the information to Dr. S for his decision. We will be keeping a close watch on her liver, so if a problem does develop with the statins, we should see it early enough to take corrective action.

We also ask Dr. S about the potential long term effects of having high BUN and creatinine numbers, and a low eGFR, all indications of kidney function, in all likelihood caused by the anti-rejection medications. He suggests that Kathy's numbers are currently acceptable, that we should get really concerned if her BUN goes above 60 (it's at ~ 40 now, which is higher than the normal of 10-20); if her creatinine goes above 2 (it's at 1.2 right now, but has been as high as 1.5); and if her eGFR goes below 30 (it's ~ 40 right now). We'll keep track of all this.

December 24-27 – We travel to visit my mother for Christmas. Our kids are staying home to be with the grandkids; or are so far away that they're simply not coming home this Christmas. So, we travel to see my mother. My brother Randy and his wife Linda also join us.

It's a great weekend and a beautiful white Christmas. We get six inches of snow, some of it while we're traveling there. It's been years since the four of us joined Mom for a Christmas at home, since long before Dad passed away. There's lots of teasing and joking, even more eating, and a little card playing. My brother and I take a long walk through the snow covered hills. The air is fresh and it's a walk that's both invigorating and tiring. Kathy, Linda, and Mom are content to stay home. All in all it's a great time. Traveling home was uneventful.

December 28 – We go to a friend's birthday party locally. It's his 60th. We enjoy the evening very much.

December 29 – We finally receive Kathy's lab work from the tests done on December 20th. Her numbers are much better, with white count and red count either normal or nearly normal. Apparently the effects of the allopurinol have dissipated. We go see Dr. H3, Kathy's nephrologist. He's pleased with the latest lab tests, particularly that her creatinine is now down around 1.2. He advises that as long as we can keep it near that, Kathy's kidney's should be just fine, so long as the other numbers, BUN, eGFR and uric acid, do not deteriorate further. Later, he advises us that her uric acid is 6.3, nearly in the normal range of around 2.4 – 6.0. At this point we believe the cherry extract she's been taking, a homeopathic, non-prescription medication, is in fact helping to reduce her uric acid. And, it's not nearly as dangerous as the allopurinol is to Kathy.

December 30 – Our handicapped kids are come for a visit and lunch today. We enjoy the day.

December 31 – It's a quiet day, in spite of the coming new year. We're just not ones to stay up late and celebrate. It's a sign of our age I suppose. Sleep is more important than partying.

January 1-5 – These are mostly ordinary days, except for going to Probate Court on January 3rd to have Kathy's mother's will probated. It's a fairly straightforward process, since her will is simple, leaving her assets in equal amounts to her four daughters; and the assets are below the amount that requires any detailed inventory or very much accounting. It's still sad however. When we're out shopping or on errands, I still have to catch myself before suggesting that we stop by to see her mother.

On January 4, we finally receive a recommendation that Kathy take a 10mg daily dose of pravastatin, a drug that reduces cholesterol by interfering with an enzyme (HMG-CoA reductase for those that care to know) that facilitates cholesterol production. Dr. S sends us a prescription.

I begin to review the potential side effects for the medication. Google is a great tool for this, or drugs.com. We already knew about the risk that any statin poses to Kathy's new liver. What we didn't know was that in combination with cyclosporine and niacin, it also increases the risk of myopathy, a loss of muscle mass and function, and/or rhabdomyolysis, severe musculoskeletal toxicity, either of which can result in severe damage to the kidneys through the production of a protein called myoglobin.

The reports indicate that cyclosporine increases the blood level of pravastatin by five to ten times above what it would be without the cyclosporine. Fortunately, this did not show any adverse effects in a group of some 100 transplant patients. However, Kathy had been drinking over a liter a day of a flavored, zero-calorie, vitamin-supplemented water per day which also provided over two grams of niacin per day, well in excess of the daily minimum, and well over that recommended when combined with the pravastatin.

So, we immediately reduce her consumption of this specialized water to no more than 20 ounces per day, limiting her niacin consumption to one gram per day. At some point we may reduce it to zero, just to minimize the risk.

January 6 – Kathy starts her pravastatin.

January 7-16 – These are pretty ordinary days, except for the continuing cold weather and snow. So far Kathy hasn't experienced any obvious side effects from the pravastatin. She continues to do her walking and routine daily activities. On January 15th we attend a swim meet for one of our granddaughters. She does exceptionally well, setting new personal bests, and wining four of the five events in her age group. We're really proud. Afterward we go to the local aquarium and enjoy the exhibits. Kathy does just fine with the travel and all the walking around. We arrive home tired, and sleep well.

January 17 – Kathy has her blood work this morning. We'll soon see if the pravastatin in combination with her other medications is having any early effect on her liver or muscular system. We should also know whether her bile duct function is improving since the stents are no longer in place. We're both eager and anxious to see the data.

January 18-20 – Normal days doing normal things. We attended a girl's high school basketball game on the 18th. Our friends Sue and Lendelle have a foreign exchange student from Spain named Gracia, living with them, who is a starter on the team. It was an exciting game, which they won in overtime by one point. It was the most excited I have seen Kathy at a sporting event. A year ago, it was hard to imagine her attending such an event, let alone getting excited and into the event.

January 21 – We get the results from the first blood test since Kathy started the pravastatin, and they're generally good. Her liver function continues to be well within normal parameters.

Her kidney function has deteriorated slightly, but is within the normal range. She needs to drink more water, and I had mentioned this to her a few times over the past month. It's really hard to be disciplined about drinking extra water when you're just not thirsty. But, she must!

January 22-31 – These are good days with a couple of good weekends, going to a movie, visiting friends, and a little shopping. During this period, we travel by car to Charleston, SC, where I had some business, but it's also a place that Kathy loves to visit, and where we have several good friends. January 28th is also Kathy's birthday. So, it's great to see Kathy enjoying these kinds of trips and activities, particularly on her birthday in a place she's likes so well. Though she still tires easily, she also recovers pretty quickly, and continues to return to her normal enthusiastic self.

At this point, I'm going to suspend the narrative. Kathy is doing well, though we must still manage her kidney and liver function, and her cholesterol level, something we're determined to do.

She is still at a greater risk for contracting a debilitating disease than the general population. She's also still at significant risk from the various complications of a liver transplant. Recall that some 10-15% of people die in the second through fifth years after the transplant.
But, she's alive and doing well, and we're going to work really hard to make sure she stays that way, managing all the things we need to manage. We hope our sharing of our story will help you do the same.

To be continued… one day at a time. Each day is a blessing.

Getting to Normal 17

We work every day on getting back to normal, but *normal is different for us now.*

Some years ago, Kathy had brain surgery to remove a tumor called an acoustic neuroma, and she became totally deaf in her left ear, and lost any sense of balance provided by that ear. Normal was re-defined for us then. She had to get accustomed to not hearing well since she had no hearing in one ear. Through an extensive rehabilitation effort, she had to learn to walk and drive again, and to do all the routine things we normally take for granted, with only one sensory capability for balance and hearing.

I had to learn that she couldn't detect the direction of sound; and I had to learn to tell her specifically where I was in the house when she called me. Saying "Here," didn't help, since sound had no sense of direction for her. She had to become accustomed to constantly feeling a bit dizzy, because of the loss of balance in one ear. She continues to deal with tinnitus, since there is now a constant ringing or roaring in her ears. At night she goes to sleep with the TV on, and set to go off after she normally falls asleep. My new normal is getting accustomed to having the TV on to allow her to go to sleep. Normal was re-defined by her new physical limitations, in many ways for both of us.

Normal is once more being re-defined, again for both of us. I feel a greater sense of tenderness and patience toward her. We have always gotten along really well and I've always felt great tenderness toward her and been generally patient with anything that might bother me.

Rare was the time when we had a fight – that being defined as a time when we did not want to speak to one another. We've never yelled at one another, and rarely even raised our voices in frustration. Having nearly lost her, my feelings for her are simply more tender and patient.

I'm also more on edge now, ever the worry wart. Even at the slightest indication of her being ill, I tend to go on "alert". I hope this is a good thing, so long as I don't panic. Kathy has to caution me not to overreact at times. I'm learning to live with this state as a part of our new normal.

Normal now includes disciplined twice daily medications every 12 hours, along with a daily check of her vitals, i.e., blood pressure and temperature. Normal now includes regular blood work to check her liver and kidney function, to check for anemia and leucopenia, and most importantly to check for rejection and other parameters that are vital to her continued health.

Normal now includes washing all fresh fruit and vegetables with a vegetable wash; and not eating raw seafood (not that she ever liked sushi or oysters anyway); and not eating salads or anything from a salad bar or any of these kinds of things at a restaurant because we do not know if they have been properly cleaned. Normal now includes cooking everything fully at home, to at least 160F, to minimize the risk of infection, and using a thermometer to check meat temperature.

Normal now requires that anyone visiting us use a hand cleaner as soon as they enter our home; and we carry hand cleaner with us at all times and use it routinely. I hope people at church don't think too poorly of us as we clean our hands after the "sign of peace" during mass, which usually includes a handshake or hug.

Normal now includes a trip to the ER at *any time* she has a fever above 101.5, since her risk of serious infection and even death is now much higher with the immuno-suppression induced by the medications.

Normal includes being in "quarantine" after I return from a trip. Since Kathy is susceptible to infection, I don't kiss her for three days after I return from a trip, just to make sure I'm not infected and could pass something along to her.

Normal now includes entering into a spreadsheet and tracking all her blood work on a regular basis to check for any trends or abnormalities in her condition. These are all normal things for us now.

And of course, normal has always included the normal things everyone does, such as preparing meals, doing dishes, doing laundry, cleaning house, doing yard work, visiting with friends and family, and last but not least, working. Kathy has resumed these kinds of normal activities. Normal now includes truly enjoying working with her in cooking, cleaning, and all the chores that we do every day, even shopping. She's also resumed the job of keeping the company books, as well as our handicapped children's, and our personal accounts.

She's doing all these things normally. Neither of us knew how much we would actually enjoy these routine tasks until she was not able to do them. Normal now includes enjoying the little things that I used to consider boring or mundane. You never know how much you can enjoy those until you can't do them together.

We continue to be hopeful for her and our future living our new normal lives together.

Epilogue – Summary of Fifty Lessons Learned

18

One essential characteristic of modern life is that we all depend on systems – assemblages of people or technologies or both – and among our most profound difficulties is making them work. In medicine, for example, if I want my patients to receive the best care possible…a whole collection of diverse components have to somehow mesh together effectively. Anyone who understands systems will know immediately that optimizing parts is not a good route to system excellence.

Dr.'s Atul Gawande and Donald Berwick

Sometimes, when I think about the past couple of years in general terms, it all seems like a bad dream that happened many years ago and is now barely visible in my mind, shrouded in a foggy mist. At other times, specific events or moments will come to mind, and they seem as clear as if they happened yesterday, and the fear or sadness of that event swells within and I relive it. Those moments are the worst, and at times bring tears to my eyes, or put a knot in my stomach. Kathy has less recollection of those very difficult times, and that's probably a good thing.

Our journey has been a long and difficult one, especially for Kathy who has suffered through it all and met each challenge with determination. It began in earnest with a hypoglycemic event, and went from there to chasing diabetes, and then on to a biopsy and an endoscopy.

Encephalopathy and aphasia ensued shortly thereafter on several occasions, as she battled high blood ammonia levels. The testing for qualifying for a transplant was exhausting as she grew weaker. When she was finally approved for a transplant, her blood sodium was critically low, risking heart failure or a stroke, and requiring immediate hospitalization and treatment. This corrective treatment resulted in her brain stem swelling, and related encephalopathy and aphasia. After getting her blood sodium in reasonable control, she underwent the transplant which went well, receiving an excellent liver. Discharge followed a week later.

Three days later she had a grand mal seizure induced by one of the more modern anti-rejection medications. Re-hospitalization ensued, brain hemorrhages were discovered, and changes were made to her medications. Biopsies were done to check for rejection. After this, she embarked on a long slow path to recovery. These were dark times. After being discharged again, her rehabilitation progressed, but was interrupted by anemia and leucopenia, along with two hospitalizations for a high fever, and another biopsy to check for rejection, all harrowing events. It was a long period of time. We're now cautiously optimistic.

The Transplant Center has thus far done an excellent job, along with all the related doctors. We would not hesitate to recommend them to anyone in need of a transplant, particularly a liver transplant. Being new to the area of liver transplants as we were, there were many things we wish we had known beforehand. We captured those lessons learned as our story unfolded. They are summarized below, beginning with the broader, at times more philosophical, lessons, and then followed by the more specific ones. These are the many lessons we've learned thus far, and there will likely be more in the future. We continue to work hard for a good outcome for Kathy, though the risks to her are still significant.

Broader Lessons Learned

Doctors, hospitals, and medical professionals live in a highly competent world of certain imperfection. This observation is illustrated below. Constant vigilance is essential.

- Instructions from the Transplant Center provide good guidance for assuring survival until the transplant, a good transplant outcome, and as rapid a recovery as reasonably possible. All instructions and guidance should be followed to the maximum extent possible, and with exceptional discipline. However, you must be aware of your condition as a patient, or as a care giver, of the patient's condition. There are many variables that can affect the outcome, so it's essential to be engaged in the process and to constantly be aware of the patient's condition, asking questions and seeking guidance along the way. Some treatment and instructions may need to be modified, as they did with Kathy, as you move through the process.

- We found that many doctors often do not think at a systems level. We have so many specialists today, and Kathy was treated by many of these, including a gastroenterologist, cardiologist, pulminologist, hepatologist, surgeon, neurologist, hematologist, nephrologist, and perhaps others. This is a good thing, having people who have in-depth experience in specific body systems and diseases allows for treatment of the most difficult of these diseases and having a positive outcome. One not-so-good consequence is that this tends to lead to a situation that a doctor friend of mine calls "splintered medicine". That is, no one is looking at the person as a complete system, thinking of all the potential consequences of each specialist's recommendations and decisions. And, more critically, a situation in which contraindicated orders can be given. Our observation of this was recently validated by an Australian study that concluded "…there's been a rising concern for some time in medical circles that doctors are becoming so super-specialized, they sometimes recommend treatments that make less sense when considering the other conditions afflicting the patient, beyond that particular doctor's area of interest." One example with Kathy was being on aldactone while on a low sodium diet, resulting in her blood sodium becoming critically low, and potentially deadly.

As a patient or caregiver, you must be alert to asking questions when different specialists order different procedures and medications. Beyond Kathy's critically and very dangerously low blood sodium level, also recall the nephrologist ordering allopurinol for Kathy when she was on azathioprine. These are contraindicated. The Transplant Center team did a reasonably good job of integrating these issues. That is, they acted as a team and by and large made good decisions to assure the best outcome for Kathy. Still, there was considerable room for improvement in integrating all the issues, medications, and orders to achieve an even better result for Kathy.

I often felt helpless on this issue. I wasn't medically trained, but felt like I had to make sure that all the orders and medications being given by all the specialists were consistent with each other and that none were contrary to any other. Granted the doctors did most of this, and did a good job. But, they weren't perfect, as is discussed in Kathy's story.

Nonetheless, over time I developed a set of questions that helped, and I offer them for your consideration and use. Each time the team came into Kathy's room I had 5-10 questions for them to help me understand what they were doing, and to help Kathy and me do what we needed to do to help her and the doctors. In general, these questions follow the pattern outlined below, with specifics added to give proper meaning to the issue at hand:

1. From the previous day's activities and Kathy's symptoms or condition, I would provide specific information about these, and ask about the meaning of these, any reasons for concern, and if any action might be necessary, by her, by me, or the doctors.
2. Regarding tests or medications, I would ask:
    a. What specifically are you ordering?
    b. Why are you ordering this? That is, what is the expected outcome from this (test, medication, procedure, etc.)?
    c. What are the risks in doing this? What are the risks in not doing this? How will we know if these things are happening, or not?
    d. How effective is the medication? Are there any common side effects to be aware of? Any rare, but serious side effects that we need to be aware of? Any interactions with other medications she's on to be aware of?
    e. How accurate is the procedure? How often do you get a false positive? How often does the test miss something?
    f. Is this (test, medication, procedure, etc.) consistent with the other diagnoses and orders for her? That is, is anything

you've ordered inconsistent with those, or will it put her at greater risk if done? If not done?

Generally doctors will be considering these issues when they order something, but they can forget, and that can be a serious oversight. It doesn't hurt to ask questions and be as well informed as possible.

- Doctors can be wrong a significant percentage of the time (see the TV drama House for examples). Their diagnosis is based on standards that relate to symptoms and test results. Unfortunately, the human body is very complex, and the same symptoms can be related to any number of diseases or conditions. This problem only increases with the complexity of the disease. So, their diagnosis is their best guess with the information they have. It's essential to constantly check to see if the diagnosis and treatment are working and consult your doctor if you believe they are not.

- Diagnostic tests can also be wrong a significant percentage of the time. For example, one ultrasound for Kathy incorrectly diagnosed a major arterial blockage that was **not** present, while another diagnosed no bile duct blockages when a significant one **was** present. Ultrasound is routinely used because it is the least intrusive and lowest risk procedure, but it appears to be incorrect a high percentage of the time. It is essential to understand the statistical accuracy rate of all the tests done, and to act accordingly, that is, being more alert to and questioning those tests that have the highest statistical error rate.

- Drug side effects and interactions are not given nearly enough review and consideration, and this can lead to major complications, including death. Drug interactions generally require much more attention than most doctors are willing, or even able, to provide. There are literally thousands of drugs on the market, and millions of drug interactions. Recall, for example, Kathy's seizure from the tacrolimus; the effect of combining azathioprine and allopurinol on both red and white blood count; the effect of both micophenolate mofetil and valganciclovir on her red and white blood count; and the interaction of niacin with pravastatin to create a potentially toxic situation for muscle and kidneys, and the risks thereto. It's essential to review drug side effects and interactions, to ask questions, do your own research on this issue, and act accordingly.

- It's important that doctors know you're actively engaged in reviewing the information available. It's a bit like raising children, that is, if they know you're watching, they behave better. If doctors know you, or your advocate, are actively participating in your or your patients healthcare, they will pay more attention, and do a better job. It's just human nature to do so. During Kathy's hospital stay, I had questions every day for the transplant team that related to Kathy's condition, behavior, symptoms, etc., sometimes as many as 10-15 questions. They always came prepared.

- It is essential that you actively review and verify all the medications and decisions being made, particularly during a transition, e.g., transfer to another part of the hospital, discharge to home, dealing with a new technician, nurse, or doctor, etc. *Double check everything.*

- It's important to challenge any inconsistency in instructions, both instructions for the patient, and orders for the hospital staff. Ask questions. Both patient and care giver must be fully engaged in the treatment and recovery process. Before and after surgery, the care giver has the primary responsibility to be an advocate for the patient, since the patient will still be recovering and under the influence of multiple medications, and may not be competent to do this.

- Hospitals have protocols that they require the staff to follow for treatment and care of their patients. At times, however, these are not followed in patient treatment. That was the case for Kathy when she was immunosuppressed and being treated for an infection. The protocols were clearly posted outside her room, but not being followed. If you observe this happening, do not hesitate to ask why the procedures aren't being followed, and if necessary, challenge the hospital staff to change their practices, both verbally and in writing. Your health and well-being is in fact their first priority, and good hospitals will respond accordingly.

- We found that our insurance company was very helpful, not the money-hungry underhanded demons that so many in the movies, national news media, and politics want to portray them. In fact they were quite the opposite, being very caring and helpful. They did, of course, advise us about what was covered under our policy and what was not. They covered what they said they would cover, and did not cover what they said they would not. That's fair. Any time we had a question, they were very responsive in providing detailed and accurate information. It's essential that you understand your coverage for any given procedure at any given institution.

- It is inconceivable to me that a transplant patient can cope with all the things that need to be done without a full-time care giver. And, in the first month or two after the transplant, the primary care giver will need help in dealing with all the work that needs to be done and issues that need to be addressed. It's an exhausting, all-consuming effort to be there 24 hours per day, 7 days per week. If you're a primary care giver, you'll need help so you can get a little rest from time to time.

- Twice since her discharge from the Transplant Center, Kathy has had a very high fever of 103F, and both times there was no clear diagnosis as to cause, only speculation. The simple fact is that doctors don't understand every cause of every illness.

- Kathy's blood level of cyclosporine varied from 58, or non-therapeutic and risking rejection, to 509, or toxic. This happened while she was adhering strictly to the transplant center protocols, and her daily dose only varied from 300-500mg per day. That's an 877% variation in blood level, with only a 67% variation in dose. Her doctors could not explain why this occurred. The body sometimes does mysterious things that doctors simply can't explain.

- It will likely take months, maybe even a year, before the transplant patient begins to feel like their old self again. We were told this, but it's not real until it happens.

Specific Lessons

Now, the more specific lessons, which were:

- Kathy changed doctors for her liver disease. In one instance, the doctor apparently did not review her previous medical file. This turned out to have a potential negative consequence to Kathy's diagnosis and treatment. The lesson –

- When changing doctors, it's essential to ask the new doctor if he or she has reviewed your file and has reached any conclusions regarding this review; whether any new treatment is indicated; or any discontinuation of treatment is indicated. The doctor should also be asked to explain each decision or recommendation.

- One doctor diagnosed auto-immune hepatitis, but **without** a biopsy, a standard protocol for this diagnosis. Another doctor did several tests, including a biopsy and endoscopy, and diagnosed primary biliary cirrhosis. The final diagnosis that resulted from studying Kathy's liver once it was surgically removed was auto-immune hepatitis. The lesson –

  - Even the best tests can be interpreted incorrectly, particularly when the diseases are closely related, such as auto-immune hepatitis and primary biliary cirrhosis. So it may be important to assure that all the tests provide for a consistent diagnosis. That said, a proper diagnosis requires proper testing. (An incidental lesson - even a blind hog can find an acorn every now and again.)

- Two doctors independently said it was ok for Kathy to be on a low dose of sleeping aid and an anti-depressant, even with her liver disease. This resulted in Kathy having an event of encephalopathy in March, 2009 and an automobile accident. She didn't even remember running over a curb, having a blowout or damaging her car. Her liver wasn't processing the medications, resulting in a much reduced cognitive ability. The Lesson –

o If you have end-stage liver disease, avoid any sleep inducing or psychotropic medication, unless you're under the *immediate* supervision of a medical professional. And, do not drive. It's dangerous.

- The hepatologist didn't limit or monitor protein consumption during Kathy's end-stage liver disease, and the Transplant Center dietician encouraged a high protein diet of 60-75 grams per day, along with 1,700 calories to maintain Kathy's strength. Her gastroenterologist had instructed her to limit her daily protein consumption to 40-45 grams per day. For her weight, this should be enough to minimize muscle mass loss *and* minimize the risk of developing high blood ammonia levels and its associated encephalopathy. After seeing the hepatologist/liver expert and Transplant Center dietician, Kathy went on a high protein diet, and within two days had an encephalopathic event, and an even more severe event two days later. After reducing her protein consumption back to 40-45 g/day, she did not have any further events from high blood ammonia. The lesson -

    o If you have end-stage liver disease, be very careful about protein consumption. A minimum amount is required, but excess protein can increase blood ammonia levels and result in encephalopathy and aphasia. While this may not be true for everyone, it is something to be very cautious about and to monitor daily.

- Related to his, one doctor had Kathy on aldactone to reduce edema, or fluid buildup in her body. Simultaneously, the Transplant Center dietician prescribed a low sodium diet, not to exceed 2,000mg per day, but without prescribing a minimum level for daily sodium consumption. Given Kathy's illness and lack of appetite, this combination resulted in her blood sodium declining over a month to a critically low level of 107. This level could have resulted in any number of serious or even deadly conditions. The transplant team quickly worked to correct her low blood sodium. This resulted in brain stem swelling, more fluid build up around her heart and lungs, and encephalopathy. The lesson –

  o Be very careful about taking aldactone (or any diuretic) and going on a low sodium diet. If you do, set a lower limit for sodium consumption, and monitor blood sodium levels frequently, e.g., weekly, to minimize the risk of critically low blood sodium.

- Kathy had several ultrasounds done. In one case, the ultrasound test of her carotid artery indicated a >70% stenosis or blockage. A more accurate testing technique, a CT Scan, indicated little or no blockage. Another ultrasound test on her bile duct indicated there were no blockages. This indication also turned out to be wrong, after an ERCP showed considerable blockage. One ultrasound test indicated a blockage that didn't exist; another indicated no blockage when it did exist. The lesson –

  o Ultrasound testing apparently has a high rate of being inaccurate. However, it is often the *least invasive test* that can be done, and thus is often given priority by doctors. Just be aware that they can be inaccurate.

- Kathy's MELD score varied significantly over a period of six months going from essentially no score to a very high score and varying in between. The lesson –

    o The MELD Score can vary considerably during a very short period, and is not a precise measure. While it may be the best measure currently available for setting liver transplant priorities, it appears to be in need of improvement. One suggestion is to "peg" each of the components of the MELD Score at its highest level, since it certainly isn't going to get any better. Doctors, clinicians, and statisticians far wiser than me should work on this, if they are not already.

- We worked really hard to make sure we did things correctly, often repeating instructions to make sure we understood. We found that while this minimizes error, even it sometimes doesn't work. For example, I repeated the instructions given to me for Kathy's breathing exercise, saying "10 times per hour, 10 times?" What I should have said is "10 times an hour, 10 *breaths* each time?" Then the nurse could have corrected me. The lesson –

    o The fact that you've repeated an instruction does not mean you understand it and can do it correctly. This probably applies for all situations, that is, being as succinct and descriptive as possible to make sure everything is done correctly.

- Contrary to clear instructions not to combine sleeping pills and wine, I tried to do so. The lesson –

- Do *not* take a sleeping pill and then try to drink a glass of wine in bed, especially if you're really tired. It's a lot like taking a sleeping pill and a laxative and going to bed. The results will not be good.

- My observation of Kathy after she was discharged immediately following the transplant was that something was wrong. Her dose of anti-rejection medication had been increased by more than 50% the day of discharge. Over the next three days, she routinely stared into space in a trance-like state for long periods of time, and only responded fuzzily when spoken to. Moreover, she had severe trembling, and flailed wildly when she put any physical effort into, for example, getting out of the shower, or even getting into bed. In fact I had suggested to the nurse coordinator that Kathy may have had a mini-seizure early on a Monday morning before the grand mal that afternoon. These symptoms were dismissed as "normal". Then she had the grand mal seizure. The lesson –

  - Some trembling is normal in the first few weeks after a transplant. When it becomes "wild" under very mild physical effort, it may suggest that a seizure is imminent. Moreover, we learned later that staring into space in trance-like state, as Kathy did shortly after her discharge from the hospital, can be an indication of a form of seizure in some people. If these happen, be alert for a pending seizure. It may be necessary to be more assertive with your doctor.

- On a few occasions, Kathy made statements like "I don't think I'm going to make it, or I'm dying", after receiving bad news, or after being unable to do certain things that she had been able to do before the surgery. While this is common, given the trauma of the surgery and the overall condition of the patient even prior to surgery, try to be calm in the face of it, particularly be alert to the medications and their influence, especially prednisone. The lesson -

- o Prednisone induces emotional swings. This is only amplified when you get bad news (like having a CMV infection and needing even more medication), and are really tired (which is common, especially with the physical therapy), and you're in constant pain from the surgery/medications. Be prepared to manage these, either by being supportive and encouraging; or by giving a "buck up" speech – you're going to make it. Selecting the right approach is a difficult judgment call.

- I began reading to Kathy as part of her rehabilitation, and as a substitute for her enjoying reading, since she was unable to read for several months. The lesson –

  - o Read to your spouse or loved one at bedtime, or other times. It will make for good conversation, but more importantly, fond memories.

- The neurologist recommended that Kathy *not* be given citalopram, an anti-depressant that had been prescribed previously and implicated in problems related to lethargy, but the transplant team ordered citalopram. Then the hepatologist stopped it three days later, after she became increasingly confused, though likely because of the effect of the cyclosporine. The lesson –

  - o While the increasing confusion is likely related to other medication, it may not be appropriate to take other psychotropic or mind-altering medications simultaneously. In matters related to potential depression and the use of anti-depressants, exercise caution and rely more heavily on the neurologist's opinion.

- The transplant team did not think that Kathy's swollen brain stem would cause her problems with chronic coughing. Later, in speech therapy, the therapist noted that people who have had swollen brain stems often have problems with their throat and swallowing, and with coughing. The lesson –

  o Brain stem swelling can cause chronic coughing and difficulty swallowing, but so can the anti-rejection medications. It's essential to have a speech therapist involved in analyzing, diagnosing and providing a therapy regimen in instances of brain trauma.

- Nausea can be a constant problem in the first few months after surgery, and sometimes before. Kathy was nauseas daily for months after her surgery.

  o Kathy at times objected to taking the anti-nausea medication, but she learned to take it and it helped minimize the symptoms and get her through many days.

- Kathy's appetite was very whimsical for a long period of time, and she often had little or no appetite. The doctors said she could eat anything she liked for the first few weeks. The dietician seemed to be working more from a script, i.e, eat heart healthy, rather than looking at the individual's condition and working on a program over time that was specifically designed for her current condition, and then tracking that progress over time. Further, our instructions were to strictly avoid eating raw food, and particularly that served in a restaurant, like sushi, salad or the salad bar, but Kathy was often served salad (leafy salad or cole slaw) in the hospital, which is institutionally prepared food as well. The lessons –

- o While this was not an immediate lesson, after her surgery and discharge we quickly learned to let Kathy eat anything she wanted and could keep down in the first few months, as the doctors had suggested. It took some nine months after her transplant for her to truly regain her appetite and eat a heart healthy diet consistent with the dietician's recommendations.
- o Avoid raw food of any type, even in the hospital. It would be nice if the hospital food service coordinated with the transplant doctors to assure consistency with doctor recommendations. We did this ourselves.
- o Avoid anything in a restaurant that is made with mayonnaise. Mayonnaise is made with eggs and can quickly become contaminated with bacteria.

- After surgery, Kathy's blood glucose level was monitored four times daily using the standard pin prick blood test with a glucose meter. The purpose was to check for and manage the onset of diabetes, a common occurrence in about 15-20% of transplant patients. If her glucose level was high, the appropriate units of insulin were given. Following discharge, we were instructed to continue to measure her glucose level four times daily – before breakfast, lunch, and dinner and at bedtime. We did so, and her glucose levels were typically normal, a good sign. When she was re-admitted following the seizure, the hospital staff did not continue with these checks. I asked about this, noting the inconsistency in orders. They started checking again, initially doing it four times per day, then two times per day, and then discontinuing it, after her levels were routinely demonstrated to be in the normal range. After she was discharged from the hospitalization for the seizure, the nurse coordinator advised us to do the check before breakfast (fasting), just as a precaution. The lesson –

- o It's critical to question any inconsistency.

- The greatest risk of error is during any transition period, making mistakes much more likely. For example, this occurred with Kathy's medication at discharge from the rehabilitation hospital, when the pharmacy delivered medications that were inconsistent with her discharge orders. The lesson –

- o Double check everything, especially during a transition period.

- When the doctors changed Kathy's primary anti-rejection medication to cyclosporine, she initially reacted poorly to the dose being given, developing encephalopathy and aphasia. When the dose was reduced, she tolerated the lower dose much better. Then the dose was increased to the initial dose, one that had been toxic to her, and she tolerated it well. The lesson –

- o The patient may be able to tolerate a high dose of cyclosporine or other anti-rejection medication, even though earlier that same dose had induced encephalopathy and aphasia. Apparently reducing the dose and then slowly increasing it allows the body to adapt to the medication and tolerate it reasonably well. The doctors had no explanation of why this happens, only that it does.

- Keeping track of medications is very difficult, but essential and requires exceptional discipline. Several lessons were learned over many months, so there was no real "Aha" moment. They are –

  o Use the medication sheets provided by the Transplant Center and shown in Appendix H to facilitate the discipline needed to keep track of them. This is critical, particularly since they can change weekly, and sometimes even daily.

  o Set up weekly doses in a pill container, and double check these as you fill each dose of the medications. We made mistakes as we were filling the pill container (e.g., leaving a pill out or putting two in one box) and double checking caught it. Double checking is also important because changes often occur mid-week, adding to the complexity and the likelihood of making a mistake. Double and triple checking will minimize that risk.

  o Set your clock (cell phone clock or other clock) to alarm twice daily at the appointed times as a good technique to avoid missing or delaying a dose.

  o Keep with you, both patient and caregiver, a listing of current medications at all times. You never know when hospitalization will be required and this is critical information to the doctors. This is also difficult, since they can change so frequently. A sample listing of medications, similar to one that we always have with us, is provided in Appendix I

- All the medications have side effects, some of which are serious. Some of the medications require that when stopping them, it be done gradually. For example, in one instance the PA indicated Kathy could stop one of her blood pressure medications, metoprolol, "cold turkey", but we found later, after noticing that Kathy's heart rate immediately jumped by 30 beats per minute from ~80 to ~110, and after reading the medication sheet, that it should have been done gradually. Doctors and medical staff may not always be aware of, or remember to, advise you on common side effects or protocols – there are literally thousands of medications and they simply can't track them all. Said more simply - doctors, and PA's, and nurses can sometimes forget to do the things they know to do. It's important to understand each medication's side effects and how to stop the medication. The lesson –

  - o Read the medication information sheets provided. This is a tedious and boring task, but also essential. Ask the doctor appropriate questions regarding any side effects; and about discontinuing any medications – should it be done gradually, and if so how? It's important to back them up with your active participation in and knowledge of your treatment.

- While the frequency of change has declined over time, Kathy's medications have changed over 40 times since her transplant. At times they change weekly and sometimes twice weekly, depending on the blood work and her progress, or lack thereof. We also paid for her medications out of pocket, which is very expensive. Her pre-transplant medications were suspended, and thus were of little benefit post-transplant. Her tacrolimus was suspended after the seizure, and we had just bought some $2,000 worth. Her micophenolate mofetil was suspended, and we had some $1,000 worth on hand. Her valganciclovir was suspended and we had some $3,000 worth on hand. The list goes on. There are a few lessons here –

- o If your insurance does not cover medications or is limited in this regard, you should be prepared to spend thousands on medications. Knowing this, it's probably best, if the logistics of your situation support it, to buy in small lots to minimize the amount of waste incurred.

- o The medications are constantly changing as your body adjusts to its new liver, or as your body becomes intolerant of a given medication and requires another. It is critical to keep an active medications list and stay on top of the medications prescribed. Discipline and compliance are essential.

- Many of medications can destroy your red blood and white blood count, e.g., micophenolate mofetil and valganciclovir. These should be tracked closely, and as you approach critical levels, a transfusion and/or other medications may be indicated to stimulate red or white blood count. Some of the medications made Kathy anemic and neutropenic, and we were not aware of the criteria for becoming concerned or taking action. Kathy's hematologist later advised us that a transfusion is indicated when the hemoglobin measure goes below 7, or hematocrit goes below 21. Either can indicate severe anemia. Neutropenia, or severe risk of infection is indicated when the white blood cell count for absolute neutrophils go below 1. This should become part of the standard information provided to families of transplant patients. The lesson –

- o Pay very close attention to these parameters and if/as they approach these levels, question your doctor about the need to take any preemptive action to minimize your risk, i.e., transfusions or medications to stimulate red and white blood cell formation.

- Being in your home environment and having friends and family around is very therapeutic. While it is tiring, it stimulates the body and mind, and accelerates a return to normalcy in both. The lesson –

- o It should be done as soon as it is safely and reasonably possible.

- Before, during, or after a transplant, you're likely to have several transfusions (Kathy had transfusions before her transplant, some 35 units during the transplant, and several units after the transplant). As the number of transfusions increases, the risk of an allergic reaction increases. To minimize the risk of an allergic reaction, pre-treatment may be necessary, e.g., acetaminophen, benadryl and/or a shot of about 50mg of steroids. If the patient has had few transfusions, no preparatory work may be necessary. Further, IV's tend to have a volumetric effect on blood count, that is, the more IV's the greater volume of blood. The lessons–

- o Be cautious about blood transfusions post-op. Make sure the doctor considers the need for pre-treatment before any post-op transfusion, especially after you've been discharged to go home, where your current doctors may not fully appreciate this need.

- Also be aware of the diluting effect of IV's, given they are done post transfusion. They tend to lower the absolute numbers for blood counts because of the increased volume in your blood.

- Going into a hospital is a transition, particularly in going to a non-transplant hospital, and therefore a period of higher risk of mistakes, so you may want to insist on maintaining direct control of all medications related to the transplant. The hospital staff may not be comfortable with this, but the rationale is:

  - The hospital may not handle transplant patients and not be familiar with the medications required.

  - You do not want to risk that they may change brands of anti-rejection medication. Different brands have different efficacies and the Transplant Center advises not to change brands.

  - Hospitals tend to give medications in certain two hour bands of time (or longer if they are really busy with emergencies). You want to make sure you adhere strictly to taking your medications to your schedule to maximize consistency in dosing and blood levels of medications.

- A high fever can induce febrile encephalopathy and/or aphasia. It's critical that the transplant recipient and care giver be aware of this. The lesson –

  - Anytime that even a slight fever is indicated, extra caution must be exercised to make sure appropriate treatment is given in a timely manner. Steps must be taken to reduce the fever, e.g., doses of acetaminophen and/or benadryl, and more frequent measures of temperature and blood pressure must be taken, e.g., hourly or even half-hourly . If or as the condition worsens, hospitalization may be required.

- Kathy had been on a relatively constant daily dose of anti-rejection medication for several months when she developed daily headaches, and substantially increased jitteriness and trembling. It turned out that the level of cyclosporine in her blood had become toxic, that is, outside the therapeutic range, requiring immediate adjustment of her dose. The lesson –

  o If you unexpectedly develop symptoms of daily headaches, and substantially increased jitters and trembling, get your blood checked to see if there's been an increase in the cyclosporine level to greater than 400.

- On at least one occasion, Kathy had a substitute technician take blood for her tests. The technician showed up late, had difficulty locating Kathy's orders, and even had difficulty getting her computer booted up to locate her orders. We told her three times that Kathy was a liver transplant patient, and needed a complete red and white blood count, liver function and kidney function, plus GGT and cyclosporine levels. When the results came in, the blood count was incomplete, and no liver function was done, but, a hepatitis screen test was done. The lesson –

  o If a substitute technician is taking blood and has difficulty finding the orders for the lab work to be done, along with similar characteristics to those listed above, be sure to ask the technician to *repeat back to you* the tests that are being done, *before* she takes the blood samples; or go to another lab. Indeed, repeating the tests being done back to any technician is a good idea.

- A nephrologist ordered a low dose of allopurinol for Kathy to lower her uric acid and minimize the risk of developing gout. No mention was made of the risk of its effect on lowering both her red blood and white blood count. After researching the side effects and drug interactions of allopurinol, we found that it should not be taken with azothioprine. Or, if it is, blood count monitoring must be done more frequently. But, this was after we asked. The lessons (re-learned) –

  o Each doctor sees the patient from the view of his specialty, and can order things that are contraindicated relative to other orders, or require special attention to a parameter that did not require much attention. The patient and/or caregiver must make sure that each doctor's orders are consistent with all other specialists' orders.
  o Medication side effects and interactions require detailed review and constant vigilance.

- When Kathy's gastroenterologist ordered a low dose of pravastatin, neither the transplant center nor her doctor mentioned of the interaction of niacin or cyclosporine with pravastatin and the risks thereto. Taking these in combination puts the muscular system, and more importantly, the kidneys at substantial risk, and must be managed. The lesson, again –

  o The issue of drug interactions, and reviewing all the doctors' orders at a systems level, both require constant vigilance.

- I travel a lot on business, including to foreign countries, meeting and coming in contact with hundreds of people. This, of course, exposes me to any number of pathogens. While I'm less susceptible to disease, Kathy is obviously much more susceptible to infection and disease. The lesson –

  - If you travel and have a spouse significant other that has had a transplant or has a suppressed immune system, we recommend that you exercise extra caution, e.g., more frequent washing of hands, not kissing nor having other intimate contact for several days after returning from a trip. If you're infected, it should show up in the first few days after your exposure, and thus allow you to avoid passing it on.

Finally, one last lesson, our mantra, that I'll repeat one last time, which helped us get to today - *take it all one day at a time*, while maintaining a high degree of vigilance and looking to the future with hope and anticipation.

We hope our sharing of our story will help you in your journey.

Appendices

Listing of Medications – Trade and Generic Names

The following is a list of medications that Kathy has taken at one time, or is currently taking. Copyrighted trade names are listed first, with the generic name listed second.

1. Aldactone – spironolactone – for minimizing fluid buildup in the body
2. Ambien – zolpidem – for sleeping
3. Bactrim – sulfamethoxazole and trimethoprim – an antibiotic
4. Celexa – citalopram hydrobromide – for depression
5. Cellcept – micophenolate mofetil – an anti-rejection medication
6. Cholac – lactulose – minimizes fluid buildup
7. Colchesine – colchesine – to enhance liver function
8. Corgard – nadolol – for lowering blood pressure
9. Darvocet – acetamenophin & propoxyphene napsylate – for pain
10. Fortaz – ceftazidime – an antibiotic
11. Gengraf – cyclosporine – an anti-rejection medication
12. Imuran – azathioprine – an anti-rejection medication
13. Keppra – levetiractum – for minimizing the risk of seizures
14. Levaquin – levofloxacin – an antibiotic
15. Lopurin – allopurinol – reduces uric acid to minimize risk of gout
16. Monistat – miconazole – an antifungal for vaginal itch
17. Mycostatin – nystatin – an antibiotic
18. Neomycin – neomycin – an antibiotic
19. Neupogen – filgrastim – for stimulating white blood count

20. Norvasc – amlodipine – for lowering blood pressure
21. Pravachol – pravastatin – for lowering cholesterol
22. Prednisone – prednisone – an anti-rejection medication
23. Prevacid – omeprazole – for acid reflux
24. Procrit or Epogen – epoetin alpha – for stimulating red blood count
25. Prograf – tacrolimus – an anti-rejection medication
26. Toprol XL – metoprolol succinate – for lowering blood pressure
27. Tylenol – acetaminophen – for pain
28. Urso Forte – ursodiol – for enhancing bile duct and liver function
29. Valcyte – valganciclovir – for treating cyclomegalovirus
30. Vancocin - vancomycin – an antibiotic
31. Xifaxan – rifaximin – an antibiotic, typically used in treating diarrhea
32. Zofran – ondansetron – for nausea
33. Zosyn - piperacillin and tazobactam – an antibiotic

Daily Dietary Log-
Example

Below is a direct copy of a daily log sheet that Kathy used to track protein (P), fat (F), Carbs (C), and Calories (Cal). Glucose was tracked daily, as well as weight. She signed the log each day as a test for any encephalopathy that might be developing.   A shaky signature would indicate potential onset of encephalopathy.

			P	F	C	Cal
June 2, 2024	Mary Kathleen _____					
WT 143.6						
4:16A BS 73 (Glucose) 6:10A BS 110						
4:16A Nutri Grain Bar			2	3	23	130
Coffee						
½ c Oatmeal			5	3	27	150
2 t Honey					8	30
snack 1 g Cracker			1	1	12.5	80
2 t P. Butter			2	5	2	60
1 Applesauce ½ c			0	0	12	50
1 c Salad 1 cup Dressing			0	1.5	4	25
Lettuce, Tom, Carrot			0	1	1	14
3/4 Wheat Thins			2	6	21	140
3 oz Tuna (Albacore)			7	.5	0	35 689
			18			
¼ c Cottage Cheese			6	1.25	3	45
½ c Mixed Fruit			1		14	50
1 Rice Bran			3	1	14	70
Rice Cakes			1	0	13½	60
½ c Rice Bran			31	9	19	150
½ c Skim Milk			4		6	35
2 g Cracker			2	2	25	120
1 T. P. Butter			3.5	3	35½	95
			48.5	42	189	1314

Monthly Summary of Daily Food Consumption-Example

C

Aug	P	F	C	Cal's	Na	Comments
1	45	34	208	1280		
2	57	28	201	1175		
3	36	19	158	980		
4	39	25	152	985		
5	48	36	132	1025		Met TC dietician-Increased Protein; low sodium diet
6	59	42	285	1730	1470	
7	60	32	295	1565	1210	
8	54	33	268	1550	850	To ER; released
9	57	46	264	1660	1160	Hospitalized w/ encephalopathy
10	4	0	73	300	260	
11	44	19	377	1830	1215	
12	42	12	310	1495	1025	
13	40	29	246	1435	1425	Walked 5 min; light weights
14	39	36	274	1550	1130	
15	43	24	227	1255	885	
16	42	36	203	1290	880	Walk; weights
17	43	35	276	1575	1480	Walk; weights
18	40	28	271	1460	900	Walk; weights
19	40	24	273	1455	1345	Walk; weights
20	41	36	277	1545	1135	Walk; weights
21	17	8	191	860	590	
22	38	20	237	1280	800	
23	32	16	248	1225	1115	
24	33	23	164	1015	1160	
25	43	14	236	1185	1050	
26	44	30	253	1455	920	
27	23	18	171	920	840	Threw up a.m.
28	38	40	170	1185	1055	
29	36	22	179	1070	955	
30	38	22	154	965	865	
31	14	10	98	500	370	
Avg	40	26	222	1251	1003	

World Health Organization- Safe Surgery Checklist[1]

D

Based on extensive research of some 4,000 patients in both the reference database and in the test database, and using eight hospitals in eight different countries ranging from richest to poorest, the World Health Organization Safe Surgery Checklist has identified three fundamental areas and 19 specific checks shown below that are required to reduce complications and risk of death. These checks have been demonstrated to reduce all complications by 36%, infections by nearly 50%, and deaths by 47%:

1. Before anesthesia, there are seven checks:
    a. Verify the identity of the patient.
    b. Verify that permission has been granted by the patient for the surgery.
    c. Verify the surgical site is marked.
    d. Verify the pulse oximeter (measures patient oxygen levels) is on the patient and working.
    e. Check the patient's medication allergies.
    f. Review the risk of airway problems, and that any needed counter-measures are available.
    g. Check for the possibility of more than half liter of blood loss and verify that necessary intravenous lines, blood and fluids are ready.

2. Before the incision, there are seven checks:
    a. Each surgical team member is introduced by name and role.
    b. Confirm that they have the right patient, and procedure, including which side of the body the surgery will occur.

c. Confirm that antibiotics were given on time, or were unnecessary.
d. Check that any radiology images needed are displayed.
e. Discuss the critical aspects of the case, e.g., length of operation, blood loss to prepare for, and anything else considered critical.
f. Review the anesthesia plans and concerns.
g. Nursing staff reviews the equipment availability, sterility and any concerns regarding the patient.

3. At the end of the operation, there are five checks. The circulating nurse reviews verbally:
   a. The recorded name of the completed procedure for accuracy.
   b. The labeling of any tissue specimens going to the pathologist.
   c. Whether all needles, sponges and instruments have been accounted for.
   d. Whether any equipment problems need to addressed before the next case, and who will follow up on this.
   e. The surgical team reviews aloud their plans and concerns for the patient's recovery, to ensure information is complete and clearly transmitted.

In the base or reference data, some 4,000 patient surgical procedures were reviewed with over 400 patients experiencing complications, half of which were infections, and a quarter of which were technical failures requiring a return trip to the operating room to stop bleeding or repair a problem. Further, in this reference database an average of 67% of the hospital surgical teams *failed* to perform one or more of these very simple, and routine required checks. Even in the very best hospitals, six percent failed to do at least one of the steps – that's one in every 16 patients. Dr. Gawande also related specific incidents regarding how the checklist saved his patients from serious harm and in one case, death.

While these may seem too simple, and perhaps even annoying to some, they have been demonstrated over and over to work, in the airlines industry, in manufacturing plants, and as demonstrated here, in surgical procedures. Checklists are not to teach people what to do, but rather to *make sure they do what they know to do*.

1. Source: The Checklist Manifesto by Dr. Atul Gawande, Metropolitan Books, Henry Holt and Company, New York, NY, 2009.

Temporary Relocation –

Packing/Moving To-Do Checklist

Get packing boxes and pack:
- Knives and cutting board
- Scales – food, people, postage
- Measuring cups
- Storage containers
- Cleaning supplies
- Printer
- Office supplies – pens, paper, print cartridges, batteries
- Office supplies – stamps, stapler, checkbooks, files,
- Headset for webinar
- Clothing of course for fall and winter
- Books – MCSCP, Tools, Others
- Personal items
- Meds – Kathy's and mine, including albuterol
- Exercise gear
- Small tool kit – flashlight, screwdrivers, hammer, pliers, and wrenches
- TV Ears

Put away:
- Grill
- Truck
- Pillows/cushions on deck

Tasks:
- Change air filters
- Re-set thermostat
- Clean Fridge; turn off small one
- Forward phones
- Leave lights on – with timer?
- Re-route mail – premium forwarding
- Stop paper – News Sentinel and Farragut Press
- Contact bank

Ask Ron to pick up any "stuff" that ends up in our paper or mail box
Ask Liz to check house once per month
Cut grass
Ask friends to cut grass when needed
Fix fridge leak
Empty fridges – both
Muscle relaxant – get prescription in case of back seizure
Refill all prescriptions
Pick up laundry
Empty trash
"Seal" all sinks/tub drains with water; cover drains
Haircut
Turn off computers
Turn off big TV
Set alarm

On Arriving:
Notify everyone of the new temporary mailing address and other info, like phone numbers, hospital name and location, etc.

Vitals Check List- Example   F

Wt. is weight; BP is blood pressure; HR is heart rate; T is temperature.

Date	Wt.	BP(am)	HR	T(am)	BP(pm)	HR	T(pm)	Glucose

Daily Activity Journal- Example

G

Date	Notations	Activity
Time		
6:00		
7:00		
8:00		
9:00		
10:00		
11:00		
12:00		
1:00		
2:00		
3:00		
4:00		
5:00		
6:00		
7:00		
8:00		
9:00		
10:00		
Other Comments		

Weekly Medication-
Checklist Example

Name: **DOB:**   **DOE:**   **MRN:**   **Allergies:**
Date: (Month)   **Day:**

Medication	Dose	Time	Su	Mo	Tu	We	Th	Fr	Sa
Cyclosporine 100 mg – Teva Only Anti-rejection	1cap	8am							
Cyclosporine 100 mg – Teva only	1cap	8pm							
Cyclosporine 25 mg – Teva only	3cap	8am							
Cyclosporine 25 mg – Teva only	3cap	8pm							
Azathioprine 50mg Anti-rejection	1 tab	8pm							
Valganciclovir 450 mg Treats CMV	1 tab	8am							
Levetiracetum 500mg Anti-seizure	1 tab	8am							
Levetiracetum 500mg	1 tab	8pm							
Ursodiol 500mg Bile Duct	1 tab	8am							
Prednisone, 5mg Anti-rejection	1 tab	8am							
Sulfamethoxazole/ Trimethoprim 400mg/80mg Prevents Infection	1tab, 3x per wk	8am							
Amlodipine, 10mg Controls BP	1 tab	8pm							
Metoprolol, 50 mg Controls BP	1 tab	8pm							
Acetamenophin/ Propoxyphene Napsylate 650mg/100mg Treats Pain	$\leq$4/day	PRN							
Ondanestron, Omeprazole, Benadryl, etc.	$\leq$ As needed	PRN							

Listing of Daily Medications – Example

I

The following is a listing of typical medications. We both keep a list of Kathy's current medications with us *at all times*. As noted above, Kathy can become encephalopathic when her fever goes above 102, and so as her care giver, I need to have a listing with me as well.

Example Listing of (Person) Meds @ (date)

Medication	Dose, Time
Cyclosporine	125mg, 8am
Cyclosproine	100mg, 8pm
Cellcept*	500mg, 2x per day, 8am&8pm
Prednisone	5 mg, 1x per day, 8am; w/food
Valcyte	900mg, 2x per day, w/food
Metoprolol	100mg, 1x per day (blood pressure)
Norvasc*	10mg, 1x per day (blood pressure)
Bactrim*	400-80mg, 1x on M, W, F @8am
Acifex*	20mg, 1x per day, 8pm
Darvocet	650/100mg, PRN, NTE 4/day
Acetaminophen	500mg, PRN, NTE 4/day
Odansetron	4mg, PRN for nausea
Amoxicillin*	2000mg, 1x before dental work
Immodium*	PRN, NTE 16mg/day (@2mg x2)

Benadryl, Robitussin & Musinex, PRN, all non "D"
* Generics are acceptable

About the Author

Ron Moore lives with his wife Kathy in Knoxville, TN, where they are employees of The RM Group, Inc., a manufacturing management consulting firm. They were high school, then college sweethearts, but parted ways. To make a long story short, they came together again some 20 years later, and now have between them six children and 13 grandchildren. Ron has a BS and MS in mechanical engineering, along with a MBA, while Kathy has a BA in art. Their very different perspectives, combined with their very similar values, provide balance in their relationship, and ultimately make for a very kind and loving life together.

10276841R00159

Made in the USA
Charleston, SC
22 November 2011